A WORD IN SEASON

A WORD IN SEASON

AN ANTHOLOGY OF READINGS FROM THE FATHERS
FOR GENERAL USE

Editor
HENRY ASHWORTH, O.S.B.

Assistant Editors
ANNE FIELD, O.S.B.
MARY BERRY, C.S.A., M.A., PH.D. (CANTAB)
EDITH BARNECUT, O.S.B.
ROSEMARY MCCABE, M.A. (CANTAB)

VOLUME I
ADVENT — CHRISTMASTIDE

DUBLIN 1973
THE TALBOT PRESS

THE TALBOT PRESS LIMITED
P.O. Box 43A
Ballymount Road
Walkinstown, Dublin 12, Ireland
SBN 85452 098 8
First published 1973

ACKNOWLEDGEMENTS

The translation of St John of the Cross in Monday, Second Week of
Advent is by E. Allison Peers (Burns Oates 1934).

The Dogmatic Constitution of the Church, for Tuesday, Second Week
of Advent is taken from the C.T.S. edition.

Designed by Liam Miller
Set in Pilgrim type and printed in the Republic of Ireland
at the Dolmen Press, Dublin

PREFACE

> The books to be read at the Night Office are
> the divinely inspired books of both the Old
> and New Testaments, as also the commentaries
> on them written by the most renowned and
> orthodox catholic Fathers.
>
> (Holy Rule of St Benedict, Chapter 9)

With these observations St Benedict in the sixth century provided his monks with the best from the theologians of previous centuries and of his own time: the Fathers of the Church.

The setting is to be noted: the Fathers were to be used as part of monastic prayer, not just for private meditation and edification. From this we see the esteem in which Benedict held the Fathers. Such esteem has remained as part of the Christian tradition to our own day. For this reason a collection of the Fathers that could act as a guide to the new Gospel cycles of the Roman Mass lectionary was felt to be useful. If at times the allegorical interpretations they seem to indulge in do not fit our modern tastes, we should try to penetrate beyond their words to the rich strata of theological and spiritual perceptions underneath. It is hoped that this edition will serve as an aid to Benedictine houses in search of Patristic readings and to all those who would like to read the best of the Fathers and thus to follow more closely the new cycles of Gospel readings with the tradition of the Fathers as a guide.

We recommend these volumes to all and express our debt of gratitude to Father Ashworth and to the translators.

✝ Rembert G. Weakland, O.S.B.
Abbot Primate.

S. Anselmo,
Christmas 1972

ACKNOWLEDGEMENTS

This edition of the best of the Fathers could never have been achieved without the devoted help of the editorial board, the encouragement of the Very Reverend Dom Rembert Weakland, Abbot Primate O.S.B., and the interest and support of my own Abbot, the Very Reverend Dom Aelred Sillem, O.S.B.

My gratitude is also due to many friends, both at home and abroad, for their suggestions concerning the selections. I am under special obligation to Dom Alexander Olivar, of Montserrat, and to Dom Burchard Neunheuser of Maria Laach and S. Anselmo, Rome, in this matter.

A further debt of gratitude is due to the patience and skill of the translators; to the Reverend Douglas Carter, to Dom Leo Williamson, O.S.B., to the Reverend Jerome Hay, C.S.S.R., to Fr Philip O'Brien, O.C.S.O., to Dame Anne Field, O.S.B., and to Dame Edith Barnecut, O.S.B., of Stanbrook Abbey, to Miss Audrey Fellowes and Sister Ide Ní Riain, and also to Sister Benedicta of Fairacres, Oxford, to Walter Mitchell and Frank James, all of whom have contributed much labour and valuable suggestions in the course of translation and final editing. Finally, mention should be made of the devoted and scholarly assistance given by Dr Mary Berry and Miss Rosemary McCabe, both of Newnham College, Cambridge. It is a pleasure for me to thank both them, and Dom Placid Murray, O.S.B., of Glenstal for so much generosity.

A word of gratitude is also due to Alexander Tarbett, Managing Director of The Talbot Press, who from the first has shown much sympathy and interest in this venture. Whatever flaws there are either in the selection of these passages or in the references given are entirely the fault of the Editor.

H. A.

Quarr Abbey, Ryde,
Isle of Wight, England.

CONTENTS

CONTENTS

CONTENTS

CHRISTMASTIDE

CONTENTS

ADVENT

A reading from the Catechetical Instructions of St Cyril of Jerusalem.
15. 1-3. PG 33: 870-874.

The Two Comings of Jesus Christ

I am not going to teach you about only one coming of Christ, but also about a much more glorious second coming. In his first coming Christ gave us an example of patient endurance, but when he comes again he will bring the crown of the Kingdom of God.

You see, almost everything relating to our Lord Jesus Christ takes place in two ways. His nativity is one example, for he was begotten by God before all ages, and was also born of the Virgin at the end of the ages. So likewise his coming down from heaven : when he came first it was in obscurity, like dew on a fleece; but he is to come again, and that coming will be in full view of all mankind. The first time he came he was wrapped in swaddling clothes in a manger; when he comes the second time he will *clothe himself in light as in a garment*. In his first coming *he endured the cross, disregarding the shame*. His second coming will be in glory, with hosts of angels in attendance.

So this is why we must not let our hearts rest in Christ's first appearance among us, but must also be full of longing for him to appear again. *Blessed is he who comes in the name of the Lord* was our cry when he first came. When we meet our Lord with the angels at his second coming, we shall again cry out in adoration : *Blessed is he who comes in the name of the Lord.*

It is not to be judged again that our Saviour will come, but to bring to justice those who were his own judges. He did not say a word when on trial himself, but then he will remind those

2

wicked men of their cruel treatment of him on the cross. *These things you did* he will say *and I was silent.* Formerly he came, in fulfilment of the divine plan, to teach men by persuasion, but this time they will have to bow to his authority whether they want to or not.

Both of these comings are mentioned by the prophet Malachi. He refers to the first when he says: *And suddenly the Lord whom you seek will enter his temple;* but the description *the messenger of the covenant for whom you long* applies to the second. *Look, he is coming, the all-powerful Lord! Who will endure the day of his coming, who remain standing when he appears? For his approach will be like a refiner's fire, like a fuller's soap, and he will take his seat to refine and purify.*

St Paul also tells of these two comings: writing to Titus he declares that *the grace of God our Saviour has appeared to all mankind. It teaches us that we must not go on living without any thought of God, but must renounce our evil desires and practise self-control. While we are in this world we should live devout and upright lives, and wait for the fulfilment of that blessed hope of ours, the appearance of the glory of our great God and Saviour, Jesus Christ.* Do you notice how he mentions both a first coming, for which he gives thanks, and also a second one, for which we are waiting?

So then, according to the article of the creed which we profess, and which you have now been taught, we must believe in him who 'has ascended into heaven and sits at the right hand of the Father. He will come again in glory to judge the living and the dead, and his reign will have no end.'

Yes, our Lord Jesus Christ will come from heaven; he will come in glory at the end of the world, on the last day. For there is to be an end to this created world, and this end will herald its final restoration.

YEAR I. Mt 24 : 37-44

A reading from the Commentary of St Paschasius Radbertus on the Gospel of St. Matthew.
Ex Expositione in Matthaeum, Lib 2, cap 24: PL 120, 799-800.

Watch, so that you may be ready

Watch, for you do not know the day nor the hour. While these words are really addressed to all men, they are nevertheless spoken by Christ as though they concerned only his immediate hearers; such is the case with many other things we read in Scripture. This saying applies to all, in so far as the last day and the end of the world will come for every man on the day he departs this present life. How necessary it is, then, that the day of our death should find us in the state in which we desire to be found on the Day of Judgment! Everyone ought to make preparation against that Day and take care not to be led astray, otherwise he will forget to keep watch and the day of the Lord's coming may find him unprepared. If a man is not ready on the day of his death, then he will be unprepared on the Day of Judgment also. We must not think that the Apostles were misled into expecting the Lord to return in judgment during their own lifetime. There is no doubt, however, that they took every care not to be drawn from the right path; they kept watch and put into practice all their Master's general precepts, so that they might be found ready when he came again.

And so we too must pay heed to the double nature of Christ's coming: the one when we shall have to render him an account of all that we have done, and the other his daily coming to each man's conscience. He comes to us now, in order that his future coming may find us prepared. For what good will it do me to know the Day of Judgment, if my conscience is burdened with sin? to know whether the Lord will come, or when he will come, unless he first comes and establishes his dwelling in my soul — unless Christ lives and speaks within me. If Christ already lives in me and I in him, then all will go well with me at his second coming. If I have already died to the world and can say, *The world has been crucified to me, and I to the world*, then already, in a sense, his final coming will be present to me.

Let us consider also this other saying of his: *Many will come in my name*. None but Antichrist and his members deceitfully assume his name, though they lack the words and wisdom of Christ and the word of truth. You will never find our Lord in the Gospels actually saying: 'I am the Christ'. His teaching and miracles were enough to reveal him to his disciples, for the Father was at work in him. Louder than a thousand tongues acclaiming him, his teaching and power cried out: 'I am the Christ'. And so, though you may not hear him declaring himself in so many words, nevertheless the works of the Father and his holy teaching reveal who he was; whereas those false christs who have neither godly deeds nor doctrine swear in loud-voiced boast that they are what they are not.

YEAR 2. Mk 13: 33-37

A reading from the Sermons of St Augustine.
Sermon 18, 1-2; PL 38: 128-129.

Watch, for you do not know when the master
of the house is coming

Our God will come openly; our God will come and will not keep silent. The first coming of Christ the Lord, God's Son and our God, was in obscurity; the second will be in sight of the whole world. When he came in obscurity no one recognized him but his own servants; when he comes openly he will be known by both good men and bad. When he came in obscurity, it was to be judged; when he comes openly it will be to judge. He was silent at his trial, as the prophet foretold: *He was like a sheep led to the slaughter, like a lamb before his shearers. He did not open his mouth.* But, *Our God will come openly; our God will come and will not keep silence.* Silent when accused, he will not be silent as judge. And he is not silent now. By no means; when people of today recognize his voice and despise him, Scripture assures us that he will not be silent, he will not hold his hand. Nowadays when the divine commands are spoken of some people begin to jeer. They are not at present shown what God promises, they do not see what he threatens — so they laugh at his commands. After all, good men and bad enjoy this world's so-called happiness; good men and bad suffer from what are deemed this world's misfortunes. People whose lives are geared to the present rather than the future are impressed by the fact that this world's blessings and sufferings fall to the lot of good men and bad without distinction. If wealth is their ambition, they see it being enjoyed not only by decent folk, but also by the worst of men. If they are in dread of poverty and all the other miseries of this world, they also see that good men and bad both suffer from them. Therefore they say to themselves, 'God does not care about human affairs, he exercises no control over them. On the contrary; he has sent us into the abyss of this world, and simply abandoned us to its sufferings. He shows no sign of his providence.' Consequently, seeing no evidence that men are called to account, such people hold God's commands in derision.

Nevertheless, each man would do well to take thought even now, because when he so wills it, God looks, and he judges; he will not tolerate an hour's delay. When he so wills it, he waits. For what reason? Surely if he never passed judgment in this present life, some people would think he did not exist. But if he always gave sentence here and now, there would be nothing reserved for the Day of Judgment. That is why much is kept for that day; but in order to put the fear of God into those whose cases are deferred, and so convert them, some judgments are made here and now.

For it is clear that God takes no pleasure in condemning. His desire is to save, and he bears patiently with evil men in order to make them good. Yet we have the Apostle's warning: *The wrath of God will be revealed from heaven against all ungodliness,* and *God will reward each one according to his deeds.* The Apostle takes scoffers to task by asking them: *Do you think lightly of God's abundant goodness and his forbearance? Do you despise him and think his judgment a matter of no account because he is good to you, because he is long-suffering and bears with you patiently, because he delays the day of reckoning and does not destroy you out of hand? Do you not know that the patience of God is meant to lead you to repentance? By the hardness of your heart you are storing up wrath against yourself on that Day of Retribution,* when the righteous judgment of God will be revealed and he will give every man the reward his deeds deserve.

YEAR 3. Lk 21 : 25-28; 34-36

A reading from the Sermons of St Bernard.
Sermo 4 in Adventu Domini, 1, 3-4; Opera omnia, t. 4: edit. Cistercienses, 1966, 182-185.

Your redemption is at hand

My brothers, it is surely right that you should celebrate our Lord's coming with all your hearts, and that the greatness of the consolation which his Advent brings us should fill you with joy. Indeed one can only be amazed at the depth of his self-abasement, and stirred up to new fervour by the immensity of his love. But you must not think of his first coming only, when he came to seek and save what was lost, but remember that he will come again and take us to himself. It is my desire that you should be constantly meditating upon this two-fold advent, continually turning over in your minds all that he has done for us in the first, and all that he promises to do in the second.

It is time, brothers, for judgment to begin at the house of God. But what will be the end of those who do not obey the Gospel? What judgment will be reserved for those who do not stand up at the judgment now taking place? For in this present judgment the ruler of this world is being cast out, and those who seek to evade it must expect — indeed they must greatly fear — the Judge who will cast them out along with him. However, if we are fully judged now, we may safely await the Saviour who is to come, that is our Lord Jesus Christ, who will change our humble bodies to be like his glorious body. Then the just will shine forth so that both learned and simple may see it; they will shine like the sun in the kingdom of their Father.

When our Saviour comes he will change our humble bodies to be like his glorious body, provided that our hearts have been changed and made humble as his was. This is why he said: *Learn of me, for I am meek and humble of heart.* We may note from this text that humility is two-fold: there is intellectual humility, and humility of the affections, here called the heart. By the first we recognize that we are nothing; we can learn this much of ourselves from our own weakness. The second enables us to trample the glory of the world under our feet, and this we learn from him who emptied himself, taking the form of a servant. When men desired to make him a king, he fled from them; but when they wanted to make him undergo the shame and ignominy of the cross, he gave himself up to them of his own free will.

MONDAY

A reading from the Commentary of St Cyril of Alexandria on the Prophet Isaiah.
Book 1, 2: PG 70, 67-71.

The Vision of the Eschatological Church

In days to come the mountain of the Lord and the House of God shall be set above the mountains, lifted high above the hills, and all the nations shall come there. Truly, this prophecy has been fulfilled in these last days, that is, in the latter part of this age, in which the only-begotten Word of God has become visible to mortal men, made flesh and born of woman, in which he has restored that Judea and Jerusalem, which is the Church, presenting it to himself as a virgin wise and pure, without spot or wrinkle, but rather holy and immaculate, as it is written in Scripture.

All the nations shall stream to it and many people shall come and say, 'Let us climb the mountain of the Lord, to the house of the God of Jacob, that he may teach us his ways and we may walk in his paths.' There is really no need to go to great lengths to describe how all the nations have been assembled and have streamed together towards the Church holding one faith, since the result of these happenings will be sufficient evidence. This multitude of nations was called, not by the discipline of the Law, nor by the holy Prophets; it was above all the mystery of God's grace that brought them together, enlightening them with understanding and filling them with a desire for salvation through Christ.

First they climbed up the mountain and then they sought to have the Word of God preached to them. In their wanderings they were shown the way of the Lord, which, being the way of the Gospel, can only be embarked upon after purification through faith.

9

For those who wish to learn the way of the Lord must first renounce their past evil ways. We shall not seek out better ways unless we first renounce our previous way of life. Who was their spiritual guide in these matters? Who but God led them to recognize the truth? Who but God could persuade them to hold their earlier lives in contempt and to hasten towards these new ways? It was God who enlightened their minds and hearts, leading them to confess the faith. *For the Law will come from Zion and the Word of the Lord from Jerusalem.*

That blessed time when the nations would be called and converted was foretold by the Prophet when he said: *The God of power and might, Ruler and Lord, shall judge amongst the nations,* that is he will exercise justice and judgment towards all people. For injustice prevailed as the nations struggled to plunder each other, resorting to every kind of violence and passion. Since these evils have been removed from their midst, justice and judgment have been given by God. Under the rule of Christ, who is peace, all discord, quarrelling and warfare, all kinds of greed have ceased between the nations; and those injuries that arise from war, and that fear that causes war have been wiped out; instead, the will of Christ prevails, which tell us: *My peace I give you, my peace I leave you.*

TUESDAY

A reading from a homily of St Gregory Nazianzen.
Hom 45, 9. 22. 26. 28: PG 36: 633. 636. 653. 657. 660. 661.

O marvellous union!

The Word of God existed from all eternity, invisible, incomprehensible, incorporeal, the beginning from the beginning, light from light, the source of life and immortality. He is the impress of the divine archetype, the permanent seal, the perfect image, the expression and revelation of the Father. He, the very Word of God, now goes out to meet his own image. He clothes himself in a human body with a rational soul for the sake of my body and soul, to cleanse like by like. He becomes man in all things but sin. Conceived by a Virgin whose soul and body had been purified in advance by the Spirit (for it was fitting that every honour should attend his birth, especially the honour of having a virgin mother), he who is God comes forth with his assumed humanity, a single Being formed of two contraries, manhood and godhead, the one bestowing the divine nature, the other receiving it.

He who enriches others becomes poor; he experiences the poverty of my humanity so that I may share the riches of his divinity. He empties himself of his fullness, for a little while strips himself of his glory that I may have part in his plenitude.

How explain this wealth of divine goodness, this mystery that centres upon me? I had a share in the divine image but did not preserve it. He now shares in my humanity in order not only to save that image, but also to make my body immortal. A second time he enters into communion with us, a communion far more wonderful than the first.

Man was to be sanctified by the manhood of God. This was ordained for his own honour by the Father, who intended to overpower the tyrant by main force, free us, and lead us back to himself through the mediation of the Son, who shows obedience to him in all things.

So the good Shepherd, who lays down his life for his flock, comes searching for his lost sheep, finds the stray, and lifting it on to those very shoulders that bore the wood of the cross, carries it back to the life of heaven.

The Light that outshines all others follows the light of his precursor; the Word follows the voice; the Bridegroom follows the bride's escort, who had prepared for the Lord a people to be his very own, purified by water for the reception of the Spirit.

God had to become man and be put to death in order to give us life; we have been put to death with him in order to be purified. But since we have died with him we have also risen with him; since we have risen with him, we also have a share in his glory.

WEDNESDAY

A reading from the Sermons of St Bernard.
Sermo 5 in Adventu Dni, 1-3. Opera omnia, edit. Cist., 4 (1966), 188-190.

The intermediate coming of our Lord
and the three-fold renewal

We know a three-fold coming of the Lord. His third coming is as it were midway between the other two, and in it those who know him will sleep in bliss. The other two are outwardly visible, but not this one. In the first coming he was seen on earth and lived among men, when, as he himself bore witness, *they both saw and hated him*. In the final coming, *all flesh shall see the salvation of our God*, and *they shall look on him whom they pierced*. But the intermediate coming is a hidden one, in which they alone who are chosen see him in themselves, and so their souls are saved. In the first coming, therefore, he comes in the flesh and in weakness; in this intermediate one, he comes in spirit and power; in the last, he will come in glory and majesty. And so this intermediate coming is as it were the way by which we travel from the first coming to the last. In the first, Christ was our redemption; in the last, he will appear as our life; in this, he is our rest and consolation, so that we *sleep between the sheepfolds*.

If anyone thinks that what we say about the intermediate coming is our own invention, let him listen to the Lord himself:

If anyone loves me, he says, *he will keep my words, and my Father will love him, and we shall come to him.* Now I have read elsewhere, *If anyone fears God, let him do good;* and I feel that there is something more in this phrase concerning the loving and keeping of his words. Where are his words to be kept? Surely in our hearts, as the prophet says: *I treasure your words in my heart, lest I sin against you.* This is how the word of God is kept, and *blessed are those who keep it.* Therefore let it pierce the very depths of your soul, let it run through your affections and your conduct. Eat what is good, and your soul shall delight in rich fare. Do not forget to eat your bread; do not let your heart grow dry, but come and let your soul be filled as with a banquet.

If you keep the word of God in this way, there can be no doubt that God in turn will have you in his keeping. The Son will come to you with his Father; the great Prophet will come who is to restore Jerusalem, and who makes all things new. The effect of this coming will be that *as we have borne the image of the man of dust, so we shall bear the image of the man of heaven.* As the old Adam permeated the entire human race and took possession of all, so Christ will gather to himself the whole of mankind, whom he created and redeemed, and will hereafter wholly glorify.

THURSDAY

A reading from the Commentary on the Diatessaron of St Ephrem the Deacon.

Cap 18, 15-17; SC 121, 325-328.

Be watchful, for he shall come again

In order to prevent his disciples from questioning him about the hour of his coming, our Lord Jesus Christ went on to say: *But of that day and hour no one has knowledge — not even the angels in heaven, nor even the Son.*

It is not for you to know the day or the time. This he has hidden from us so that we should be watchful and should all believe this coming will happen during our own lifetime. Had the time of his coming been revealed, then his advent would have been in vain and the nations and the ages in which it was to happen would not have yearned for it in faith. He said that he was coming, but he did not make it clear at what precise moment, so that every generation and age might long for him. Even though he made known the signs of his coming, we cannot clearly tell the day of their accomplishment, for in ever-changing manifestations these signs come and go and are always with us.

His second coming is like his first : many prophets and upright men longed for the sight of him, thinking he would appear in their own day; so too, every believer of our own time hopes to live to welcome him, especially as he did not clearly state at what moment he would appear, and this above all so that none should think him subject to a decree or to a day, when he is the one who ordains time and sequence. How then can the time of his coming be hidden from him, for he himself decreed it and described the signs that would herald it? He drew their attention to these signs, so that from the very beginning every nation and every age should believe that the coming of Christ might well happen in their own day.

Be watchful, for when the soul is overpowered by the weary burden of weakness and sorrow the enemy takes charge and can sway it to suit his will. This is why the Lord spoke of watchfulness, to prevent the soul from succumbing to spiritual numbness; for it is written : *Let righteousness awaken you!* and again : *I am risen, and here I am, present with you,* and again : *I beg you, then, not to relax your vigilance,* and further on : *Seeing we have, by an act of mercy, been entrusted with this apostolate, there must be no weakening on our part.*

FRIDAY

A reading from the 'Proslogion' by St. Anselm.
Cap. 1: Opera omnia, Edit. Schmitt, Seccovii, 1938, 1, 97-100.

The desire to see God

Come now, you poor creature, turn your back on your busyness for a little while; for a few moments leave the tumult of your thoughts, throw off the burden of your cares, and put aside your wearisome occupations. Make some time for God, rest in him for a while. Enter into the chamber of your mind, exclude everything but God, and what will help you find him; shut the door and search for him. Now tell him how you long to see his face. Say to him : *Lord, it is your face that I seek.* Say it with your whole heart.

Come then, Lord my God, come and instruct my heart where and how to search for you, where and how to find you. Where shall I look for you, Lord, if you are absent and not here? And if you are everywhere, why are you not visible to me? But of course, your dwelling is in light inaccessible. Then where is this light inaccessible, and how can I approach it? Who will guide me and conduct me into it so that I may see you? And then, by what signs, by what visible form shall I know you? I have never seen you, I do not know what you look like, Lord my God. What is this exile of yours to do in a far off land, O most high God, what is he to do? Banished far from your presence and distressed by his love for you, what shall your servant do? With burning desire he strives to see you, and your face is very far from him. He longs to come to you, and your dwelling is inaccessible. He wishes to find you and has no idea where you live. He wants to search for you and he does not know your face.

O Lord, you are my Lord and my God, and I have never seen

you. You have made me and remade me and bestowed on me all the good that I possess, and still I do not know you. In a word, I was created to see you, and I have not yet done what I was created to do.

O Lord, how long? How long, Lord, will you forget us? How long avert your face from us? When will you be mindful of us and hear us? When will you give light to our eyes, and show us your face, and give yourself to us once again? Look upon us Lord, listen to us, enlighten us, show yourself to us. Give yourself to us again so that all may be well with us, for without you, nothing is well with us. Look kindly upon our labours, our strivings to come to you, for apart from you, we can do nothing.

Teach us to seek you, and to those who seek, reveal yourself; for we can neither seek you unless you show us how, nor find you unless you reveal yourself. Let desire inspire our search, and our search strengthen our desire; let love lead us to find you, and finding crown our love for you.

SATURDAY

A reading from the Treatise of St Cyprian, Bishop and Martyr, on the Benefits of Patience.
13, 15. CSEL 3, 406-408.

Our hope is for things unseen

Our Lord and Master has given us this salutary advice: *He that endures to the end shall be saved;* and again, *If you are faithful to my word you are truly my disciples; you shall know the truth, and the truth will make you free.*

My dear brothers, since the hope of truth and freedom has been granted us, we must persevere in steadfast endurance so that we may attain to truth and freedom in themselves. The very fact that we are Christians gives us ground for hope and confidence, but for these to come to fruition, we must have patience.

For we are not aiming at present glory, but the glory that is to come. The Apostle warns us of this when he says: *We live in the hope that we have been saved. If this salvation were already in sight, there would be no need of hope, for one does not hope for something that can be clearly seen. But since we are hoping for what is still invisible, we must wait for it with patience.* Patient waiting is necessary for us if we are to attain our full stature, and, in God's own time, to achieve the object of our hoping and believing.

In another letter St Paul addresses the upright, who, through divine interest on their deposit of good works, are storing up for themselves treasures in heaven. They too are to be patient. *While there is still time,* he tells them, *let us do good to all men, especially to those who belong to the household of the faith. We must not grow tired of well-doing, for in due time we shall reap a harvest.*

In this way he admonishes men not to become impatient nor to falter in their efforts, for if they are led astray or overcome by temptation they may stop in mid-course on the journey towards commendation and glory. All their past labours would then be lost, and what had made a good beginning would fail to reach perfection.

Finally, in the apostle's words, patient endurance is bound up with charity. *Charity,* he says, *is magnanimous and kind; it does not envy, is not boastful; it is not easily provoked, thinks no evil, loves all things, believes all things, hopes all things, endures all things.* And in knowing how to endure all things, he concludes, charity finds the power to persevere to the very end.

In another passage he tells us to *bear with one another in love, eager to maintain the unity of the Spirit by the peace that binds us together;* and so he shows us that neither peace nor unity can be preserved unless brothers care for one another with mutual forbearance, preserving the bond of peace by means of patience.

SECOND SUNDAY OF ADVENT

A reading from the Commentary on Isaiah by Eusebius, Bishop of Caesarea.
Cap 40: PG 24, 365-368.

The voice of one crying in the wilderness

The voice of one crying in the wilderness, prepare the way of the Lord, make straight the paths of our God. This text clearly states that it is not in Jerusalem that the prophecy is to be fulfilled, but in the wilderness — I mean the prophecy that the glory of the Lord shall be seen and the salvation of God be made known to all flesh.

And indeed this was fulfilled historically and to the letter when John the Baptist proclaimed the saving manifestation of God in the wilderness of the Jordan, where in fact God's salvation was made visible. For Christ himself in his glory was made known to all when, at his baptism, the heavens opened and the Holy Spirit came down in the form of a dove and rested upon him; when they heard his Father's voice bearing witness to his Son: *This is my beloved Son, listen to him.*

Indeed, these words were uttered because God was about to come into a desert which had from time immemorial been inaccessible and impenetrable. For all the nations, in their ignorance of God, were like deserts which God's holy men and prophets had been prevented from entering.

And so that voice commands: Prepare a highway for the Word of God, make smooth his rough and pathless wastes, so that our God who is coming to us may travel along them without hindrance. *Prepare the way of the Lord*: this means the proclamation of the gospel, the new message of encouragement whose aim is that all mankind shall come to know the salvation of God.

Go up on a high mountain, joyful messenger to Zion; shout with a loud voice, joyful messenger to Jerusalem. These words follow most appropriately those quoted above and refer fittingly to joyful messengers. They are the announcement of the coming of God to men after we have heard of the voice crying in the wilderness. The mention of these joyful messengers was indeed a fitting sequel to the prophecy concerning John the Baptist.

For what is meant by Zion if not what was previously referred to as Jerusalem? This was the same mountain mentioned in the words of Scripture: *Here is mount Zion which you made your dwelling-place*, and mentioned also by the Apostle: *You have come to mount Zion.* In this context can it mean anything but the company of the Apostles, who were drawn from the ancient people of the circumcision?

This Zion is also that Jerusalem which received the salvation of God, and is itself placed high up on the mountain of God, that is, upon his only-begotten Word; to whom he gives the command to go up on a high mountain and to proclaim the joyful message. Who proclaims the joyful message if not the Evangelists? What is it to proclaim the joyful message, if not to announce, first to the cities of Juda and then to all mankind, the coming of Christ to earth?

A reading from the Sermons of St Augustine.
Sermon 109, 1: PL 38, 636.

Repent, for the kingdom of heaven is at hand

Some people, the gospel tells us, were rebuked by the Lord because, clever as they were at reading the face of the sky, they could not recognize the time for faith when the kingdom of heaven was at hand. It was the Jews who received this reprimand, but it has also come down to us. The Lord Jesus began his preaching of the gospel with the admonition: *Repent, for the kingdom of heaven is at hand*. His forerunner, John the Baptist, began his in the same way: *Repent*, he said, *for the kingdom of heaven is at hand*. Today, for those who will not repent at the approach of the kingdom of heaven, the reproof of the Lord Jesus is the same. As he points out himself, *You cannot expect to see the kingdom of heaven coming. The Kingdom of heaven*, he says elsewhere, *is within you*.

Each of us would be wise therefore to take to heart the advice of his teacher, and not waste this present time. It is now that our Saviour offers us his mercy; now, while he still spares the human race. Understand that it is in hope of our conversion that he spares mankind, for he desires no man's damnation. As for when the end of the world will be, that is God's concern. Now it is the time for faith. Whether any of us here present will see the end of the world I know not; very likely none of us will. Even so, the time is very near for each of us, for we are mortal. There are hazards all around us. We should be in less danger from them were we made of glass. What more fragile than a vessel of glass? And yet it can be kept safe and last indefinitely. Of course it is exposed to accidents, but it is not liable to old age and the suffering it brings. We therefore are the more frail and infirm. In our weakness we are haunted by fears of all the calamities that regularly befall the human race, and if no such calamity overtakes us, still, time marches on. A man may evade the blows of fortune, but will he evade death? He may escape perils from without but will he escape what comes from within him? Now, suddenly, he may be attacked by any malady. And if he be spared? Even so, old age comes at last, and nothing will delay it.

YEAR 2. Mk 1 : 1-8

A reading from Origen's Homilies on the Gospel of St Luke. Hom 22 in Lucam, 1-4; SC 87, pp 301-302.

Make straight the way of the Lord

Let us see what the scriptures have foretold concerning Christ's coming. First there is what was written of John: *The voice of one crying in the wilderness : prepare the way of the Lord, make his paths straight.* The sentence that follows points more directly to our Lord and Saviour, for it is through him rather than John that *every valley shall be filled in.* If each of us considers the kind of man he was before he believed in Christ, he will discover in his former self a deep and precipitous valley, plunging into the lowest depths. But when the Lord Jesus came and sent the Holy Spirit as his abiding representative, then all our valleys were filled with good works and the fruits of the Holy Spirit. The love of God no longer allows any such valley to remain in us, and if we have peace, patience and goodness in our hearts, not only do we cease to be valleys, but we begin to be very mountains of God.

Daily among the gentiles we see the prophecy fulfilled: *Every valley shall be filled in;* just as the casting down of the people of Israel from their former greatness means that *every mountain and hill has been brought low*. At one time that people was both mountain and hill; now it has been pulled down and laid low. *Through their trespass salvation has come to the gentiles, so as to make Israel jealous*. If you interpret these humbled mountains and hills as the powers raised up in opposition against the human race, you will not be wrong; for in order to fill in valleys of this sort, the mountains and hills — the forces hostile to mankind — must be brought down

Let us now see whether this prophecy was fulfilled at Christ's coming. The next words are : *the rugged ground shall be made smooth*. Each one of us used to be rugged ground. If we have not remained so, it is the coming of Christ to our souls which has made us smooth. Of what avail would his historical coming in the flesh be to us, if he did not also come to our souls? Let us pray that he may come daily to each one of us, so that we can say : *I live, now not I, but Christ lives in me*.

And so by his coming the Lord Jesus has smoothed out our rough places and levelled our uneven ground, so that an open pathway may be formed in our heart — a swift, clean road on which God the Father may walk. And may Christ the Lord set up his dwelling within us, saying : *The Father and I will come and make our home in him*.

YEAR 3. Lk 3 : 1-6

A reading from the Sermons of St Bernard.
Serm. 1 in Adventu Domini, 9-10; Opera omnia t. 4, edit. Cist., 1966, 167-169.

All flesh shall see the salvation of God

We must now think for a moment about the time at which our Saviour comes, for as you know it was not at the beginning, nor in the middle, but at the end of the ages that he came to us.

This was not determined without purpose; on the contrary, God in his wisdom decided that he would bring help to men only when their need was at its greatest, for he knew how prone to ingratitude were the sons of Adam. Truly, the day was already far spent and the evening drawing near; the sun of justice was already beginning to set, and its rays now gave diminished light and warmth to the earth. The light of the knowledge of God had grown feeble, and as sin increased, charity grew cold. Angels no longer appeared to men, no prophet raised his voice; it seemed as though, overcome by the great hardness and obstinacy of men, they had ceased to intervene in human affairs. Then it was that the Son of God said: *Here am I*. Eternity broke in upon the world at the moment when temporal prosperity was at its height. For to give only one example, peace among nations was at that time so universal that at a single man's bidding it was possible to carry out a census of the whole world.

We have considered who he is that comes, and to what place, and also the cause and time of his coming. One thing remains: we must earnestly search out the road by which he comes, so that we may be able to go out to meet him, as is fitting. However, as he came once upon this earth in visible flesh to work out our redemption, so he comes daily in a hidden, spiritual way to save each individual soul, as the scripture says: *The Lord's anointed is the breath of life to us*. This spiritual coming of his is shown to be hidden in the text: *Under his shadow we shall live among the nations*. So, then, surely even if the sick man is unable to go very far to meet such a great Physician, he should at least make an effort to lift his head and raise himself up a little to greet him as he approaches.

It is not necessary for you to cross the seas, nor to pierce the clouds, nor to climb mountains to meet your God. It is not a lengthy road that is set before you; you have only to enter into yourself to find him. *For his word is very near you; it is on your lips and in your heart.* Encounter him in compunction of heart and in confession of your sins, so that you may at least leave behind you the dunghill of a defiled conscience, for the Author of purity could not be asked to enter such a place.

All these things are said of that Advent in which Christ comes to each one of us, to enlighten our minds by the power of his Spirit.

MONDAY

A reading from The Ascent of Mount Carmel by St John of the Cross.
Book 2, Chapter 22. Edit. E. Allison Peers, Burns Oates 1934.

God has spoken to us in Christ

The principal reason why in the law of Scripture the enquiries that were made of God were lawful, and why it was fitting that prophets and priests should seek visions and revelations of God, was because at that time faith had no firm foundation, neither was the evangelical law established; and thus it was needful that they should enquire of God and that he should speak, whether by words or by visions and revelations or whether by figures and similitudes or by many other ways of impressing his meaning. For all that he answered and spoke and revealed belonged to the mysteries of our faith and things touching it or leading to it.

But now that the faith is founded in Christ, and, in this era of grace, the evangelical law has been made manifest, there is no reason to enquire of him in that manner, nor for him to speak or to answer as he did then. For, in giving us, as he did, his Son, which is his Word — and he has no other — he spoke to us all together, once and for all, in this single Word, and he has no occasion to speak further.

24

And this is the sense of that passage with which St Paul begins, when he tries to persuade the Hebrews that they should abandon those first manners and ways of converse with God which are in the law of Moses, and should set their eyes on Christ alone, saying: *In many and various ways God spoke of old to our fathers by the prophets; but in these last days he has spoken to us by a Son.* Herein the Apostle declares that God has been, as it were, dumb, and has no more to say, since what he spoke formerly, in part, to the prophets, he has now spoken altogether in him, giving us the All, which is his Son.

Wherefore he that would now enquire of God, or seek any vision or revelation, would not only be acting foolishly, but would be committing an offence against God, by not setting his eyes altogether upon Christ, and seeking no new thing or aught beside. And God might answer him after this manner, saying: If I have spoken all things to you in my Word, which is my Son, and I have no other word, what answer can I now make to you, or what can I reveal to you which is greater than this? Set your eyes on him alone, for in him I have spoken and revealed to you all things, and in him you shall find yet more than you ask and desire.

For I descended upon him with my Spirit on Mount Tabor, saying: *This is my beloved Son, in whom I am well pleased; listen to him.* Listen to him; for I have no more faith to reveal, neither have I any more things to declare. For if I spoke formerly, it was to promise Christ; and if they enquired of me, their enquiries were directed to petitions for Christ and expectancy concerning him, in whom they should find every good thing, as is now set forth in all the teaching of the Evangelists and the Apostles.

TUESDAY

A reading from the Dogmatic Constitution on the Church.
Lumen Gentium, art. 48.

The Eschatological Character of the Pilgrim Church

The Church, to which we are called in Christ Jesus, and in which by the grace of God we acquire holiness, will receive its perfection only in the glory of heaven, when the time comes for the renewal of all things, and the whole universe, as well as the human race, is completely united in Christ. For the universe has an intimate connection with man, and through him it reaches its destined end.

Lifted up from the earth, Christ has drawn all men to himself; rising from the dead, he has sent his life-giving Spirit upon his disciples; through the Spirit he has established his Body, which is the Church, as the universal sacrament of salvation. Sitting at the right hand of the Father, he is unceasingly at work in the world to bring men to the Church, to join them more closely to himself through her, and to give them a share in his glorious life by feeding them on his own Body and Blood. The promised restoration to which we look forward has already had its beginning in Christ. It receives impetus from the sending of the Holy Spirit and through him continues in the Church, where we also receive instruction, by faith, in the significance of our earthly life. Meanwhile, in expectation of a good future, we are bringing to completion the work in the world entrusted to us by the Father, and are working out our salvation.

The end of the ages has already reached us, and the world is irrevocably set on the renewal which is anticipated in a real way in this life. Already the Church is marked on earth by a genuine, if imperfect, holiness. The Church is on pilgrimage until the coming of the new heavens and the new earth in which righteousness dwells. In her sacraments and organisation, which belong to this life, she carries the mark of this world which will pass, and she herself takes her place among the creatures who groan in travail as they wait for the revealing of the sons of God.

WEDNESDAY

A reading from St Augustine's Commentary on the Psalms. On Ps. 109, 1-3; CCL 40: 1601-1603.

What God has promised is given to us through his Son

God appointed a time during which men were to live in expectation of his promises, and a time when his promises would be fulfilled. The time of expectation lasted from the days of the prophets until John the Baptist; the time of fulfilment extends from John the Baptist until the end.

God is faithful. He has made himself our debtor, not through receiving anything from us, but by promising us such great things. His plighted word was not enough; he desired to be bound in writing, as though giving us a written guarantee. Then, when he began to fulfil his promises, we should be able to study the plan for their implementation in the Scriptures. And so the whole period of the prophets, as we said before, was one in which the promises were foretold.

God holds out to us eternal salvation, an endless life of bliss in company with the angels, an incorruptible inheritance, everlasting glory, the beauty of his face, his holy dwelling place in heaven, resurrection from the dead with no further fear of dying. These things may be said to constitute his final promise, on which our whole effort is concentrated. When we achieve it we shall seek no more; there will be nothing more to ask for.

But even the manner in which we are to attain our end has not been concealed from us. God foretold it in advance, promising divinity to men, immortality to mortals, justification to sinners, and glory to those who are cast down.

Nevertheless, brethren, because men found it hard to believe that out of their present corruption, worthlessness and weakness, mortals compounded of dust and ashes would be put on a par with the angels, God came to the help of their faith. Not only did he give them a written document, he also appointed a mediator of his pledge. This mediator was to be neither prince nor angel nor even archangel, but his only Son, through whom he would show us the way by which he meant to lead us to our promised goal. God was not satisfied with making his Son our guide; he made him in person the way by which men should go to heaven, following his directions and walking in his steps.

The only Son of God, then, would come among men and assume their human nature, by means of which he would die, rise again, ascend to heaven, sit at the Father's right hand, and fulfil his promise to the nations. And after this it remains for him to complete his work by coming again, this time to require a reckoning of men, to separate those who are objects of retribution from those who are the objects of his mercy, to carry out his threats to the wicked and give his rewards to the just.

All these things therefore had to be foretold, prophesied in advance, and committed to writing as events of the future. Then they would cause no alarm by their unexpected arrival; rather men would look forward in faith to their accomplishment.

THURSDAY

A reading from the Sermons of St Peter Chrysologus.
Sermon 147. PL 52: 594-595.

Love desires to see God

God sees that the world is shaken by fear, and so his constant endeavour is to recall it through love. He invites it by his grace, keeps it constantly in his love, and binds it to himself in friendship.

Thus, for example, when the earth had grown old in wickedness, God cleansed it in the avenging water of the flood and called Noah to be the father of a new age. Addressing him in kindly words, he admitted him to his intimate confidence. Like a loving father, he gave him instructions concerning his immediate task, and assured him of his favour in the future. Not content merely to command, but actually co-operating in the work, he confined within one single ark the representatives of every living species. It was God's purpose that the love they found in each other's company might dispel their fear of mutual subjugation, and that what had been saved by a common effort might be preserved by a common love.

Again he called Abraham from among the heathen, made his name great, and constituted him father of believers. He accompanied him on his journey, preserved him among aliens, enriched him with goods, and honoured him as a conquering hero. He made a covenant with him, saved him from harm, graciously accepted his hospitality, and ennobled him with the posterity of which he had despaired. And all these blessings, this great sweetness of divine love, were given so that Abraham might learn to love God rather than hold him in awe; to worship him in love, not in fear and trembling.

When Jacob was in flight he reassured him in dreams. On his return journey he challenged him to a contest and grasped him in a wrestler's embrace. Again his purpose was to elicit love for the author of the struggle, rather than fear.

He spoke to Moses in the loving tone of a father, and called him to be the deliverer of his people.

Through the events we have called to mind the flame of divine love kindled human hearts and the overflowing love of God poured itself out upon the perception of men. Their minds became enamoured, and they began to desire to gaze upon God with their bodily eyes. But how could their limited human capacity take in the vision of God, whom the universe itself cannot contain? The law of love does not consider its nature, its duties, its capabilities; love is unacquainted with discretion, lacks reasonableness, knows no measure. It will not be soothed by being told a thing is impossible, nor give up hope on learning of the difficulties involved. Unless it achieves its desire it destroys the lover; that is why he follows its promptings rather than the call of duty. Love gives rise to desire, grows in fervour, and reaches out in burning ardour for what is forbidden. What more need be said?

Love cannot bear not to see what it loves; hence it was that all the saints thought little of their merits if they did not see God. And therefore the love that yearns to see God, even if it lacks discretion, has at least the zeal of fervent devotion.

This was what gave Moses the temerity to say: *If I have found favour in your sight, show me your face.* This, too, caused the psalmist to sing: *Show us your face.* And finally, even the heathens themselves make idols for the same reason, namely that in their very errors their eyes may behold the object of their veneration.

FRIDAY

A reading from the Treatise of St Irenaeus Against Heresies.
Book 5, 19, 1; 20, 2; 21, 1: SC 153, 248-250, 260-264.

Mary and Eve compared

When the Word came openly into his own, he was borne by
that creation which he himself sustains. When he obeyed by
hanging on the tree, he reversed the sin of Eve, who disobeyed
by eating the fruit of the tree. The Virgin Mary was already
betrothed to a man when she was told the good tidings by the
angel. Eve was already bound to a man when she was seduced
into eating the forbidden fruit. The truth of the angel's message
to Mary undid the evil consequences of Eve's fall.

For just as the one was seduced by the word of an angel so
that she fled from God by disobeying his word: so the other,
through the word of an angel, was brought good tidings, so that
she received God by obeying his word. And just as the one was
seduced into disobedience to God, so the other was persuaded
into obedience to God. Thus the Virgin Mary came to be the
advocate for the virgin Eve.

Everything, therefore, was restored when Christ summed up
all things in himself; he stirred up war against our enemy,
destroyed him who at the beginning made prisoners of us in
Adam, and crushed his head, just as we find God saying to the
serpent in Genesis: *I will put enmity between you and the
woman, between your seed and her seed; he shall crush your
head, and you shall bruise his heel.* For he who was to be born
in the likeness of Adam, of a woman who was a virgin, was
heralded as the one who would crush the serpent's head. And
this is the seed of which the Apostle speaks in his letter to the
Galatians: *The law was added because of transgressions till the
seed should come of which the promise was made.*

He explains this even more clearly in the same letter when he says: *But when the fullness of time was come, God sent his Son, born of a woman.* The enemy would not have been fairly overcome had not he who overcame been born of a woman. For it was through a woman that the enemy had gained the mastery over man in the beginning, setting himself up as the adversary of man.

Therefore the Lord called himself the Son of Man, renewing in himself that first Adam from whom Eve was made flesh in the form of a woman; so that just as our race fell to death through vanquished man, so also through victorious man we may rise again into life.

SATURDAY

A reading from the Sermons of Blessed Isaac, Abbot of the Monastery of Stella.
Sermon 51, PL 194, 1862-1863, 1865.

Mary and the Church

The Son of God is the first-born among many brethren, and though by nature he was one alone, by grace he reconciled many to himself, in order that they might become one with him. For to those who receive him *he gave power to become sons of God.*

Therefore when he was made the Son of Man, he made many into sons of God. And thus he reconciled many to himself, so that they might be one in his power and love; and though by their physical birth they are many in themselves, yet by their divine re-birth they are one in him.

For Christ is one, wholly and solely, head and body; he is one, of one Father in heaven and of one mother on earth; and he is both many sons and one Son. As he is both head and members, one Son and many sons, so Mary and the Church are one mother and many, one virgin and many.

Both are mothers, both are virgins: both were conceived from the same Spirit without physical desire; God the Father made both his own offspring without sin. Mary gave birth to the head without sin of the body; the Church gave life to the body, for the remission of the sins of all through the head. Both are the mother of Christ, but neither bears the whole without the other.

Therefore in the divinely inspired Scriptures, what we rightly apply universally to the virgin mother the Church, we apply individually to the Virgin Mary; and what we apply in particular to the Virgin Mother Mary, we apply in general to the virgin mother the Church; and since this language is composed from them both, the meaning is usually applied to each without distinction or differentiation.

Each is interpreted by turns as the faithful soul, the spouse of the Word of God, the mother of Christ, daughter and sister, virginal and fruitful. Therefore what is said in general of the Church and in particular of Mary, is also said individually of the faithful soul, by the wisdom of God himself, that is, the Word of the Father.

Hence the words: *I shall dwell in the house of the Lord*. In a general sense the house of the Lord is the Church, in a particular way it is Mary, and individually it represents each faithful soul. Christ dwells in the tabernacle of the Church's faith until the end of time; and he will dwell in the knowledge and delight of the faithful soul for ever and ever.

A reading from the Sermons of St Augustine.
Sermon 293, 3: PL 1328-1329.

John the Voice : Christ the Word

John is a Voice, but the Lord is the Word : *In the beginning was the Word*. John is a Voice for a time; Christ is the eternal Word at the beginning of time. Take the Word away, and what becomes of the Voice? Where there is no understanding, it is an empty noise. A wordless voice beats on the ear; it does not quicken the heart.

Now in this actual business of quickening the heart, let us observe the sequence of what happens. If I am thinking what to say, the word is already in my heart; but if I want to talk to you, I search for a way in which what is already in my heart may be also in yours.

In this search for a way in which the thoughts of my heart may be conveyed to yours and lodge there, I use my voice, and with its aid I speak to you; the sound of my voice conveys the meaning of the word to you, and dies away, but the word that the sound has brought you has reached your heart without ever leaving mine.

When the Word has reached you, does not that very sound seem to you to say : *He must increase, but I must decrease?* The sound of the Voice made itself heard as it performed its function and then died away, as if to say : *Now is my joy complete.* Let us hold fast to the Word; let us not lose that Word that has been quickened in the mind!

Do you want to know how it is that the Voice dies away and the Divine Word remains? What has now become of John's baptism? He ministered and went his way; today people flock

34

to the baptism of Christ. We all believe in Christ. We all hope for salvation in Christ: this was the message of the Voice.

For since it is difficult to distinguish word from voice, even John himself was thought to be the Word. But he knew himself to be the Voice: he would be no hindrance to the Word. *I am not the Christ*, he said, *nor Elijah, nor the Prophet. Who are you, then?* he was asked. *I am the voice of one crying in the wilderness: Prepare the way of the Lord. The voice of one crying in the wilderness:* the voice of one breaking the silence. *Prepare the way of the Lord*, as if to say: 'For my part, I make myself heard, that I may usher him into men's hearts; but he will not consent to come when I bring him unless you also prepare the way.'

What is it to prepare the way, if not to act with proper reverence? What is it to prepare the way, if not to have a humble heart? And for an example of humility, take John himself: mistaken for the Christ, he declares he is no such person and does not take advantage of this ludicrous error. If he had said: 'I am the Christ', how readily he would have been believed, seeing that he was believed in even before he spoke. But he did not say it: instead, he declared what he was, explained the difference and humbled himself.

He saw where salvation was to be found. He knew himself to be a guiding light, and feared lest a breath of pride in himself might extinguish it.

YEAR I. Mt II : 2-II

A reading from the Commentary of St Ambrose on the Gospel of St Luke.
Lib V, 93-95. 99-102. 109. CCL 14, 165-166, 167-168, 171-172.

Are you he who is to come, or shall we look for another?

John, calling to him two of his disciples, sent them to the Lord, saying : 'Are you he who is to come, or shall we look for another?'. If we take these words in their simple sense, we find they are contradicted by what has preceded them. There John recognized our Lord on the Father's testimony; now we hear him say that he does not know him. Are we to think that he recognized one who was until then unknown to him, only to declare now that he does not know the man he formerly recognized? *I myself did not know him*, he says, *but he who sent me to baptize with water said to me : 'It is he upon whom you will see the Holy Spirit descending from heaven'*. John not only believed these words; he acknowledged the Messiah who was shown him; he baptized him, he worshipped him, he proclaimed that this was he who was to come. Last of all he said: *I have seen and have borne witness that this is the chosen one of God*. After announcing: *Behold him who takes away the sins of the world*, is it really credible that a prophet of his stature could be so far in error as to stop short of believing him to be the Son of God?

Since the immediate sense of this passage would seem to be contradictory, we must look for the spiritual meaning. John, I have already told you, is a type of the Law which foreshadowed Christ. That Law was contained materially in the minds of unbelievers as if in a prison deprived of eternal light, and subsisted in hearts subject to pain and folly. For without the preaching of the Gospel, such a Law was unable to bear full witness to the divine economy. John therefore sent his disciples to Christ to obtain further knowledge, for Christ is the fulfilment of the Law. Knowing that no man can believe completely unless he hears the Good News — for although faith may have its origin in the Old Testament, it is only perfected in the New — our Lord revealed himself in answer to their questions by drawing attention not so much to his words as to his deeds. *Go, he said, and tell John what you have seen and heard : the blind receive their sight, the lame walk, the deaf hear and lepers are cleansed, the dead are raised up, the poor have the good news preached to them.* And yet these are still not the greatest of the signs which bear witness to the Lord : the fullness of faith is in his cross, his death and his burial. This is why he adds : *Blessed is he who takes no offence at me.* For the cross can give scandal even to the elect. There is no greater testimony, however, to the divinity of Christ, nothing which more clearly shows him to be something more than mere man, than that he should offer himself in sacrifice for the whole world; it is by this that he is fully revealed as the Lord. And it is thus that he is pointed out by John : *Behold the Lamb of God, who takes away the sins of the world.* Truly all this is the proof, given not just to John's disciples but to all of us, so that we who are convinced by the evidence may believe in Christ.

But what did you go out to see? A prophet? Yes, I tell you, and more than a prophet. Why should the disciples go out into the wilderness in the hope of seeing John, when they knew he was shut up in prison? The Lord is here setting John before us as a model. He prepared the way of the Lord not only in his birth according to the flesh, not only in his summons to faith in Jesus : he was also the precursor of his glorious passion. A great prophet indeed was he, in whom the whole line of prophets came to an end. More in fact than a prophet, for many there were who hoped to see the one of whom John prophesied, the one whom he saw with his own eyes, the one whom he himself baptized.

37

YEAR 2. Jn 1 : 6-8, 19-28

A reading from the Treatise on the Works of the Spirit by Rupert of Deutz.

Ex Tract. Ruperti Tuitiensis Abbatis De Operibus Spiritus, Lib 3, cap 3, SC 165, 26-28.

Among you stands one whom you do not know

John's baptism may be compared with Christ's by the difference there is between a servant and his master. The baptism which John preached was a *baptism of repentance*, but the baptism of Christ was *for the forgiveness of sins*. Through John's baptism Christ was revealed to Israel, but through his own, that is to say through his passion, he was glorified. Of his own mission John said: *I myself did not know him, but for this I came baptizing with water, that he might be revealed to Israel*. Christ, on the other hand, had already been baptized by John, and it is of his own impending passion that he is speaking when he says: *There is a baptism I must needs receive, and how I am constrained until it is accomplished!* So, then, John's baptism prepared the people for Christ's; Christ's baptism made them fit for the kingdom of God.

What, then, of those whom John baptized, exhorting them to *believe in the one who was to come after him*, and yet who died before Christ? There can be no doubt that when Jesus himself underwent his baptism of suffering, these were absolved from their sins, however heinous; together with him they entered into paradise and saw the kingdom of God. But as for those who in their hearts despised the divine plan of salvation, who refused John's baptism, and who departed this life before the aforesaid baptism of Christ's passion — their former circumcision brought these no remedy; our Lord's saving death was of no avail to them, nor did its power snatch them from the jaws of hell, because they were not numbered among those of whom he said : *For them do I consecrate myself.*

You must also know that there may have been some who had been baptized by John and remained alive until Jesus had been glorified and the good news of his death and resurrection proclaimed. Nevertheless, if *they received him not* and did not admit the necessity of being baptized into his saving mystery, then John's baptism availed them nothing. The Apostle Paul knew this when he *found some disciples and asked them, 'Did you receive the Holy Spirit when you believed?' And they said, 'No, we have never even heard that there is a Holy Spirit.' And he said, 'Into what then were you baptized?' They said, 'Into John's baptism.' And Paul said, 'John baptized with the baptism of repentance, telling the people to believe in the one who was to come after him, that is, Jesus.' On hearing this, they were baptized in the name of the Lord Jesus. And when Paul had laid his hands upon them, the Holy Spirit came upon them.*

How small a thing do we see that servant's baptism to have been, in which his disciples had not so much as heard that there was a Holy Spirit, in comparison with the Lord's baptism, which is never given without naming the Holy Spirit on equal terms with the Father and the Son! This is the baptism *which gives the Holy Spirit for the forgiveness of sins.* The name indeed is common to both; but what is signified by it in each case is something very different.

A reading from Origen's Homilies on the Gospel of St. Luke.
Hom 26 in Lucam, 3-5; SC 87, pp. 341-343.

Let us be solid buildings, which no storm can overthrow

The baptism which Jesus gives is in the Holy Spirit and in fire.
If you are one of the Lord's holy ones, you will be baptized in
the Holy Spirit, but if you are a sinner, you will be plunged into
fire. Baptism, though one and the same in form, has a two-fold
effect. Sinners who receive it unworthily incur condemnation
and hell-fire; but those who are converted to the Lord and live
a holy life in complete faith gain salvation and the grace of the
Holy Spirit. He who is said to baptize in the Holy Spirit and in
fire will have a winnowing-fan in his hand to clear his threshing
floor. The wheat he will gather into his granary, but the chaff
he will burn with unquenchable fire.

I should like to discover the reason why our Lord will have
a winnowing-fan, and the source of the wind which will blow
the light chaff hither and thither but leave the heavy grain
lying in a heap (for wind is necessary if grain and chaff are to
be separated). I suggest that by the wind we can understand the
temptations which disturb the faithful and bring to light the
chaff and the wheat among them. When you are overcome by
some temptation, do not think that it was the temptation that
turned you into chaff; it simply disclosed the stuff you were
made of, the fickleness and faithlessness which were concealed
in you all along. On the other hand, when you endure temptation bravely, it is not the temptation which makes you faithful
and patient; it merely reveals the virtues of patience and forti-
tude within you which had up till then been hidden.

Do you think, says the Lord, that I have spoken to you for
any other reason than to reveal your justice? As he declares

elsewhere, *I have humbled you and let you hunger, testing you to know what was in your heart.*

So then, the storm itself will not make your house stand firm if its foundations are of sand. If you wish to build, you must build upon rock. Then when a storm comes it will not overthrow your building, whereas the tottering of a house built on sand is proof that it is not well founded. So before any storm arises, before the wind blows or the waves swell, let us concentrate all our efforts on the foundations of our building, and build our house while all is yet quiet with the strong bricks of God's manifold precepts. Then when persecution rages and fearful whirlwinds rise up against Christians, we shall show that our house is built upon the rock which is Christ Jesus.

If anyone should deny Christ — and God forbid that any of us should do so — he must know that it was not at the moment of his public denial that his apostasy took place. Its seeds and roots had long been dormant within him; his denial only brought them into the open. Let us pray then to the Lord that we may be solid and stable buildings which no storm can overthrow, founded on the rock of our Lord Jesus Christ, to whom be glory and power for ever and ever. Amen.

MONDAY

A Reading from Abbot William of St. Thierry's Book on the Contemplation of God.
Nn 9-11; CS 61, 90-96.

He first loved us

You alone are Lord. And if you are Lord, then you must also be Saviour, since to serve you is the same as to be saved by you. For since, Lord, you are the acknowledged author of our salvation and of all the blessings showered upon your people, where else can this salvation lie but in that grace you give us to enable us to love you and in our turn to become the worthy object of your love for us? Surely, Lord, it must be that which caused you to decree that the Son of your right hand, the man you had established as your own, should be named Jesus, that is, Saviour: *for he will save his people from their sins; nor is there any other name by which we may be saved.* He taught us how to love him by first loving us, to the extent even of embracing death upon the cross for us; and by loving us so wholly aroused in us a love for him who first loved us to the very end.

And that indeed is the measure of it: you loved us first, so that we could be brought to love you in return. Not that you stood in any need of love from us; but simply because we should have been unable to reach that perfection for which you had designed us in any other way than by loving you. Therefore, O God, who in former times spoke to our fathers in many and various ways through the prophets, finally in these days you have spoken to us through your Son, through your Word, by whom the heavens were made firm and from whom all the strength and order of the universe are derived. This utterance through your Son is what is meant by your pitching your tent in the brightness of the sun, that is, in such a brilliant light that all may see and understand.

To such a length and with such intensity did you love us that you refused to spare even your only Son, but delivered him up for the sake of us all; while he, too, loved us to the extent of delivering himself up for our sake!

This, Lord, is how your Word, your omnipotent Word has dealt with us: who, *while all things were in silence,* plunged in the depths of error, came down from his royal throne to soften the harshness of sin and to plead for the tenderness of love. Whatever he said or did during his time on earth, however much he was insulted, struck or spat upon, not flinching from death even upon the cross or from the grave beyond it, he throughout remained your Word, addressing us as your Son, offering us your love and stirring up within us a response of love for you.

For as God and Maker of the human soul, how well you knew that no man can be constrained to love, but must be freely drawn to do so; and that where there is constraint, freedom can find no place; and wherever freedom is excluded, justice must of necessity be absent too. But you, Lord, who are supremely just, had a mind to save us; nor can you condemn or save unjustly. Therefore it must have also been your will that we should love you, for only by so doing could we justly find salvation. Nor could we ever love you till you yourself first made it possible for us to do so. Therefore, Lord, as your beloved Apostle says and we have also said: you must have first loved us — just as you must first love any who are to return your love. And, Lord, it is with that same love implanted in our hearts by you that we are moved to love you.

TUESDAY

A reading from the Imitation of Christ.
Book 2, cm. 2-3.

On humility and peace

Do not pay great attention to whether men are for you or against you, but consider your own actions, and take care that God is with you in everything you do. As long as you have a good conscience, God will defend you, for no man's malice can hurt the man whose help is in God. If you suffer in silence, you will see without doubt that the Lord will come to your aid; he knows when and how to deliver you, and therefore your role is to resign yourself into his hands. It is God's concern to help you, and to deliver you from all confusion. Often it is very profitable for us and keeps us more humble if others know our faults and rebuke us for them.

When a man humbles himself for his failings, he easily placates others and quickly appeases those that are offended with him. God protects the humble man and delivers him; it is the humble man he loves and comforts; he stoops down to him and gives him abundant grace, and after his humiliation he raises him to glory. He reveals his secrets to him, gently attracting him and calling him to himself. Though the humble man may suffer confusion, he is at peace, for his refuge is in God, not in the world. Do not think you have made any progress, until you have learnt to esteem yourself inferior to all.

First keep your own soul in peace, and then you will be able to give peace to others. A peaceable man does more good than one who is learned. A man who is at the mercy of his own passions turns good itself into evil, and readily believes the worst; whereas a good peaceable man turns all things to good. The man who is at peace with himself is not suspicious of others, but the man who is discontented and agitated is torn by all kinds of suspicions; he is neither quiet himself, nor will he allow others to be quiet. He often says things he ought not to say, and omits to do the things he ought to do. He is intent upon the duties of others, and neglects his own. First, therefore, have a zealous care over yourself, and then you may justifiably show yourself zealous over your neighbour's virtues.

You know well enough how to excuse yourself and put a good colour on your own actions, but you are not willing to admit the excuses of others. It would surely be more honest for you to accuse yourself and excuse your brother. If, then, you expect to be borne with yourself, bear with the failings of others.

WEDNESDAY

A reading from the fourth book of St Irenaeus 'Against Heresies'.
20, 4-5; SC 100, 634-640.

When Christ comes, God will be seen by men

There is one God, who by his Word and Wisdom made all things and set them in order. Now his Word is our Lord Jesus Christ, who in these last days became a man among men, in order to unite the end with the beginning, that is, man with God.

It was for this reason too that the prophets, having received their prophetic gift from the same Word, foretold his coming in the flesh to bring about the union and communion of God and man, according to the will of the Father. For from the beginning the Word of God had promised that God would be seen by men, would live with them on earth and converse with them. He was going to be present among his creatures for their salvation, and by making himself known to us, would *free us from the hands of all who hate us*, that is, from every evil spirit, and cause us *to serve him in holiness and righteousness all our days*. His reception of God's Spirit would thus be the means of bringing man to the glory of the Father.

The message of the prophets therefore is that God would be seen by men, and it is echoed by our Lord in the words: *Blessed are the pure in heart, for they shall see God.*

Undoubtedly, in his greatness and his inexpressible glory *no one shall see God and live,* for the Father is incomprehensible; yet in his love and gentleness, and because he can do all things, he grants even this to those who love him: he allows them to see God, as the prophets had foretold. *For what is impossible for man is possible for God.*

Of course man by his own powers cannot see God; nevertheless God can if he so wills show himself to men, to whom he chooses,

45

when he chooses, and in the way he chooses, for God can do all things. He revealed himself first through the Spirit by means of prophecy, then through the Son, in whom he made us sons by adoption, and finally in the Kingdom of Heaven he will show himself in his own being as Father. The Spirit prepares man for the Son of God, the Son leads him to the Father, and the Father frees him from change and decay, thus fitting him for the eternal life that comes to everyone from seeing God.

For just as those who see the light are within the light, bathed in its brightness, so those who see God are within God and share his glory, a glory that gives them life. Seeing God therefore is entrance into life.

THURSDAY

A reading from the Dogmatic Constitution on Divine Revelation. Dei Verbum 3-4.

The whole of revelation is consummated in Christ

God, who creates and preserves all things through his Word, gives men an enduring testimony to himself in created things. Moreover, with the purpose of opening the way to heavenly salvation, he manifested himself to our first parents from the very beginning. After their fall, his promise of redemption aroused in them the hope of being saved, and from that time on he ceaselessly kept the human race in his care, ready to give eternal life to all who seek salvation by persevering in well-doing. Then, at the time he had appointed, he called Abraham in order to make of him a great nation. Through the patriarchs, and after them through Moses and the prophets, he taught this nation to acknowledge him as the one living and true God, the provident Father and just Judge, and to wait for the promised Saviour. And so, throughout the ages, he prepared the way for the Gospel.

After speaking in many places and in various ways through the prophets, *God has spoken to us in these days last of all by a Son.* He sent his Son, the eternal Word who enlightens all men, to dwell among men and reveal to them the secrets of God's inner life. Hence, Jesus Christ, the Word made flesh, sent *as a man among men, speaks the words of God,* and accomplishes the saving work entrusted to him by his Father. As a result, he himself — to see whom is to see the Father — brought revelation to perfection by fulfilling it, and confirmed it with divine guarantees. He did this by the whole work of his presence and self-manifestation: by words and deeds, signs and miracles, above all by his death and glorious resurrection from the dead, and finally by sending the Spirit of truth. Thus he revealed and proclaimed that God is with us to deliver us from the darkness of sin and death, and to raise us up to eternal life.

The Christian dispensation, therefore, since it is the new and definitive covenant, will never pass away, and no further public revelation is to be expected before the glorious manifestation of our Lord Jesus Christ.

FRIDAY

A reading from St Augustine's Commentary on the Psalms. On Ps 37, 13-14; CCL 38, 391-392.

Your longing is your prayer

I cry aloud in anguish of heart, says the Psalmist. There is a hidden grieving which human ears cannot hear; but sometimes a man's heart is so consumed by some desire that his inner pain is outwardly expressed. When this happens, his neighbours will ask the reason, and will privately conjecture that the cause of the man's grief lies in something or other that has happened to him. Who can understand what it is, except the One in whose sight and hearing the sufferer groans? This is why the Psalmist says, *I cry aloud in anguish of heart;* for when people hear a man groaning, they ordinarily hear only the sound of his voice, not the cries of his heart.

Who, then, can discern the cause of the Psalmist's grief? Listen to his next words: *All my longing is known to you.* Not to men, who cannot see into the heart, but to you, my God, is all my desire laid bare. Does your longing lie open to him? Then the Father, who sees in secret, will give you your heart's desire. This very longing is your prayer; if your longing is uninterrupted, so will be your prayer. Not for nothing did the Apostle tell us to *pray without ceasing.* Did he mean that we were to be perpetually on our knees, or lying prostrate, or raising our hands? If that is our idea of prayer, I consider that unceasing prayer is beyond our capacity.

There is another kind of prayer, however, interior and continuous: the prayer of desire. Whatever else you are doing, if your desire is for that sabbath rest, you do not cease to pray. So, then, if you do not wish your prayer to be interrupted, do not let your longing flag. Ceaseless longing will be your ceaseless cry. Let your love fail, and you will fall silent. Who are the people whose cry is silenced? Are they not those of whom it is said, *Since iniquity has been at large, love has grown cold in the hearts of the majority of men?* Love grown cold means a heart become silent; burning love is the heart's cry. If your love is abiding, your cry will be continuous; a continuous cry is a sign of abiding desire, and abiding desire means that you are ever mindful of your heart's repose.

All my longing is known to you. Suppose this longing is known to God but not the actual cries of anguish? Impossible: the cries are simply the outward expression of inward longing. No, the Psalmist continues, *my groans are not hidden from you.* Hidden from the majority of men, they are not hidden from you.

There are times when this humble servant of God can be heard saying, *My groans are not hidden from you*, and there are other times when he seems to be laughing. Does this mean that his desire has died within him? Surely not; where there is desire, there is the groan of anguish. It may not always be audible to men, but it never fails to reach the ear of God.

FOURTH SUNDAY OF ADVENT

YEAR I. Mt I : 18-24

A reading from a Homily by the Venerable Bede.
Hom 5 in Vigilia Nativitatis Domini: CCL 122, 32-36.

A great and profound mystery

In his outline of the generations from Abraham to Joseph, the husband of Mary, Matthew the Evangelist has described in few words but complete truth the birth of our Lord and Saviour Jesus Christ. By this birth the Son of God, born in eternity before all ages, came on earth in our time as the Son of Man. It was truly fitting in every way that when God willed to become man for the sake of mankind, he should be born of none but a virgin. For when a virgin gives birth to a child, the son she bears must be none other than the son of God.

Behold, a virgin shall conceive and bear a son, and his name shall be called Emmanuel (*which means God with us*). The name of the Saviour by whom God is with us was given to him by the prophet; it is a name that signifies two natures united in his one Person. He who was begotten as God from the Father before time began is the same as he who is Emmanuel, God-with-us, conceived in his mother's womb in the fullness of time. The reason is that when *the Word was made flesh and dwelt among us*, he was pleased to take into the unity of his person the weakness of our nature. Thus, in a marvellous manner, he began to be what we are, without ceasing to be what he had always been. He received our nature in such a way that he did not lose what was uniquely his own.

Mary, then, brought forth her first-born son, the child of her own being. She gave birth to the one who was begotten of God before every creature and who, in his created humanity, exceeds all other created beings. *And she called his name Jesus.*

The name of the virgin-born child is Jesus because, as the angel had explained, he was to save his people from their sins. And he who saves from sin will also rescue us from the mental and bodily weaknesses consequent upon it. 'Christ', the anointed, is a word implying priestly or royal dignity. In the Old Testament both priests and kings are called christ, on account of their anointing with chrism or holy oil. They foreshadow the one who is true king and priest and who, when he came into the world, was *anointed with the oil of gladness above other kings*. From this anointing he is called Christ; those who share in that same anointing, that is, in his spiritual grace, are called christians. By his saving power, may he free us from our sins. As our high priest, may he reconcile us to God our Father. As our king, may he grant us the Father's eternal kingdom : for he is our Lord Jesus Christ, God living and reigning with the Father and the Holy Spirit till time flows into eternity.   Amen.

YEAR 2. Lk 1 : 26-38

A reading from an Advent Homily by the Venerable Bede.
Hom 3 in Adventu: CCL 122, 14-17.

Behold, you will conceive and bear a son

Today's reading of the gospel, my dear brothers, calls to mind
the beginning of our redemption, for the passage tells us how
God sent an angel from heaven to a virgin. He was to proclaim
the new birth, the incarnation of God's Son, who would take
away our age-old guilt; through him it would be possible for us
to be made new and numbered among the children of God. And
so, if we are to deserve the gifts of the promised salvation, we
must listen attentively to the account of its beginning.

*The angel Gabriel was sent from God to a city of Galilee
named Nazareth, to a virgin betrothed to a man whose name
was Joseph of the house of David; and the virgin's name was
Mary.* What is said of the house of David applies not only to
Joseph but also to Mary. It was a precept of the Law that each
man should marry a wife from his own tribe and kindred. St
Paul also bears testimony to this when he writes to Timothy :
*Remember Jesus Christ, risen from the dead, descended from
David, as preached in my gospel.* Our Lord is truly descended
from David, since his spotless mother took her ancestry from
David's line.

*The angel came to her and said, 'Do not be afraid, Mary, for
you have found favour with God. And behold, you will conceive
in your womb and bear a son, and you shall call his name Jesus.
He will be great, and will be called the son of the Most High;
and the Lord God will give to him the throne of his father David.'*
The angel refers to the kingdom of the Israelite nation as 'the
throne of David', because in his time, by the Lord's command
and assistance, David governed it with a spirit of faithful service.

51

The Lord God gave to our Redeemer the throne of his father David, when he decreed that he should take flesh from the lineage of David. As David had once ruled the people with temporal authority, so Christ would now lead them to the eternal kingdom by his spiritual grace. Of this kingdom the Apostle said: *He has delivered us from the dominion of darkness and transferred us to the kingdom of his beloved Son.*

And he will reign over the house of Jacob for ever. The house of Jacob here refers to the universal Church which, through its faith in and witness to Christ, belongs to the race of the patriarchs. This may apply either to those who are physical descendants of the patriarchal families, or to those who come from gentile nations and are reborn in Christ by the waters of baptism. In this house Christ shall reign for ever, and of his kingdom there will be no end. For the present life, Christ rules in the Church. By faith and love he dwells in the hearts of his elect, and guides them by his unceasing protection towards their heavenly reward. In the future life, when their period of exile on earth is ended, he will exercise his kingship by leading the faithful to their heavenly country. There, for ever inspired by the vision of his presence, their one delight will be to praise and glorify him.

YEAR 3. Lk 1 : 39-45

A reading from an Advent sermon by Guerric of Igny.
Sermo 2 de Adventu Domini, 1-4; PL 185, 1, 14-17.

Our King is coming !

Our King and Saviour is coming; let us run to meet him! *Good news from a far country,* in the words of Solomon, *is like cold water to a thirsty soul;* and he brings good news indeed who announces the coming of our Saviour and the reconciliation of the world, together with the good things of the life to come. *How beautiful are the feet of him who brings good tidings and publishes peace !* Such a messenger truly bears a refreshing draught to the soul that thirsts for God; with his news of the Saviour's coming, he joyfully draws and offers us water from the springs of salvation. In the words and spirit of Elizabeth, the soul responds to the message of Isaiah or his fellow-prophets: *Why is this granted to me, that my Lord should come to me? For behold, when the voice of your greeting came to my ears,* my spirit leapt for joy within me in eager longing to run ahead to meet my God and Saviour.

Let us too arise with joy and run in spirit to meet our Saviour. Hailing him from afar, let us worship him, saying: *We have waited for you, Lord, be our stronghold, our salvation in time of trouble.* This was how the prophets and holy men of old, filled with immense desire to see with their eyes what they already saw in spirit, ran to meet the Messiah. We must look forward to the day, so soon to come, on which we celebrate the anniversary of Christ's birth. Scripture itself insists on the joy which must fill us — a joy which will lift our spirit out of itself in longing for his coming, impatient of delay as it strains forward to see even now what the future holds in store.

I believe that the many texts of Scripture which urge us to go out to meet him speak of Christ's first coming as well as his second. This may raise a query in your mind. Surely, however, we are to understand that as our bodies will rise up rejoicing at his second coming, so our hearts must run forward in joy to greet his first.

Between these two comings of his, the Lord frequently visits us individually in accordance with our merits and desires, forming us to the likeness of his first coming in the flesh, and preparing us for his return at the end of time. He comes to us now, to make sure that we do not lose the fruits of his first coming nor incur his wrath at his second. His purpose now is to convert our pride into the humility which he showed when he first came, so that he may refashion our lowly bodies into the likeness of that glorious body which he will manifest when he comes again.

And so, my brothers, though we have not yet experienced this wonderful consolation, we are encouraged by firm faith and a pure conscience to wait patiently for the Lord to come. With joy and confidence we can say with St Paul: *I know whom I have believed, and I am sure that he is able to guard until that Day what has been entrusted to me,* until the *appearing of the glory of our great God and Saviour, Jesus Christ,* to whom be glory for ever and ever. Amen.

DECEMBER 17

A reading from the letters of St Leo the Great.
Ep. 31, 2-3; PL 54, 791-793.

The mystery of our reconciliation with God

Although we may acknowledge that our Lord, the Son of the blessed Virgin Mary, was true and perfect man, it will be of no avail to us unless we believe his manhood to be of that lineage which the evangelists attribute to him. For Matthew's gospel begins by setting out *the genealogy of Jesus Christ, son of David, son of Abraham,* and then follows his human descent in order to bring his ancestral line down to his mother's husband, Joseph. Luke, on the other hand, traces his parentage backwards step by step to the very first member of the human race, in order to show that both the first Adam and the second shared the same nature.

No doubt the Son of God in his omnipotence could have taught and sanctified men by appearing to them in a semblance of human form as he did to the patriarchs and prophets, when for instance he engaged in a wrestling contest or entered into conversation with them, or when he accepted their hospitality and even ate the food they set before him. But these appearances were but types, signs that mysteriously foretold the coming of one who would take a true human nature from the stock of the patriarchs who had gone before him. The mystery of our reconciliation with God, ordained from all eternity, was not to be fulfilled by any mere figure, but by the Holy Spirit coming upon the Virgin and the power of the Most High overshadowing her, so that within her spotless womb Wisdom might build itself a house and the Word become flesh. In this way the divine and human natures were to be united in one person, the Creator of time born in time, and he through whom all things were made brought forth in their midst.

For unless the New Man had been made in the likeness of sinful humanity and had taken on himself our ancient guilt, unless he who alone was free from sin, being one in substance with the Father, had united our nature to himself by stooping to share that of his mother, the whole human race would still be held captive under the devil's yoke. The Conqueror's victory would have profited us nothing, if the battle had been fought outside our humanity. But through this wonderful partnership the mystery of new birth shone upon us, so that through the same Spirit by whom Christ was conceived and brought forth, we too might be born again from a spiritual source; and in consequence the evangelist declares the faithful to have been *born not of blood, nor of the desire of the flesh, nor the will of man, but of God.*

DECEMBER 18

A reading from the Letter to Diognetus.
Chapter 8, 5-9, 6.

God has revealed his own love through his Son

No man has ever seen God or known him, but he has revealed himself to faith, since only through the eyes of faith is it given men to see him. He, the Lord and Creator of the universe, who made all things and assigned each its place, revealed himself because of his love for man and his forbearance. That love and forbearance have always been his; they are his now, and ever will be, for he is kind, good (indeed he alone is good), slow to anger and true.

He conceived a momentous, an amazing design, communicating it only to his Son. As long as he preserved this secrecy and kept his own wise counsel, it seemed indeed as though he took no thought for us, and did not care. But when through his beloved Son he revealed it and brought to light what he had prepared from the beginning, his gifts surpassed our wildest expectations, for they included not only a share in his bounty, but even sight and knowledge of himself.

God then had made his plans in consultation with his Son; everything was arranged in his own mind. Nevertheless, until it was time to reveal them he permitted us to go our own way, swept along by unruly passions, slaves of sensuality and lust. Why? Because he took pleasure in our sins? Certainly not. It was simply because of his forbearance. But while he set no seal of approval upon that age of lawlessness, he made use of it as preparation for this present age of righteousness. He intended, when our conduct during that former time had proved us unworthy of eternal life, to make us worthy by his own goodness. When we had shown that we could not of ourselves *enter into the kingdom of God*, his power would enable us to do so.

Accordingly, when our wickedness had reached its culmination and it was perfectly plain that we could expect its reward in punishment and death, the time God had determined arrived: henceforth he would manifest his goodness and power. O how boundless his love and benevolence! He did not hate us, reject us, or hold a grudge against us, but bore with us patiently. In his mercy he took our sins upon himself and gave his own Son as our ransom, the holy One for the unholy, the Innocent for the guilty, the Just for the unjust, the Incorruptible for the corruptible, the Immortal for mortals. For what else but his righteousness could have atoned for our sins? In whom but the Son of God alone could we lawless and impious men have been sanctified? O sweet exchange, work of God beyond our fathoming, undreamt of blessings, that the wickedness of millions should be hidden in a single good Man, and the holiness of One sanctify countless sinners!

DECEMBER 19

A reading from the third book of St Irenaeus Against Heresies. 3. 20: 2-3. SC 34: 342-344.

God decreed our redemption through the Incarnation

Whatever man has to boast of is from God; man himself is the work of God, the product of his infinite wisdom and power. As the skill of a doctor is shown in his patients, so God is manifested in men. Therefore St Paul says: *God has imprisoned all in unbelief in order to have mercy upon all.* Man, he is telling us, having forfeited immortality on account of his disobedience to God, afterwards obtained mercy and received adoptive sonship through the Son of God.

If he now, without any pride of boasting, holds fast to the true teaching concerning created things and their Creator, the all-powerful God who gave existence to the whole world; and if he also abides in God's love and in obedience and thanksgiving, he will obtain greater glory from him, a glory that will grow ever brighter until he is transformed into the likeness of the One who died for him.

For he, the Word of God, was made in the likeness of sinful flesh in order to pass sentence on sin, a sentence that would banish it from human nature. At the same time he wished to challenge men to become like himself; he bade them imitate God, placed them under the Father's obedience in order to bring them to the vision of God, and made it possible for them to know the Father. He dwelt among men and became the Son of Man to accustom men to receive God, and God to dwell among men, according to the Father's good pleasure.

Emmanuel, Son of the Virgin, the sign of our salvation, is therefore the Lord himself: he is the Saviour of those who by themselves could never have been saved. Paul proclaims this impotence of human kind when he says: *No good is to be found in my fallen nature, of that I am sure.* He says this to make us realize that the blessing of our salvation comes from God, not from ourselves. Further on, after his cry, *Unhappy man that I am, who will deliver me from this body condemned to death?* he introduces our liberator, the giver of this grace: *Jesus Christ our Lord.*

By Isaiah too we are reminded of our inability to save ourselves, and our dependence on the assistance of God. *Strengthen the weak hands and the trembling knees,* he says. *Let the faint-hearted take courage; be strong and have no fear. Behold our God will give sentence; he will come and save us.*

DECEMBER 20

A reading from the Homilies of St Bernard in Praise of the Virgin Mother.
Hom 4, 8-9; Opera omnia, Edit. Cist., 4 (1966), 53-54.

The whole world waits for Mary's reply

You have just heard, blessed Virgin, that you are to conceive and bear a son, not by human intervention, but by the power of the Holy Spirit. The angel who delivered this message to you is waiting for your reply, for he wants to carry it back without delay to the God who sent him. We too, on whom the sentence of condemnation weighs heavily, await your words of mercy, blessed Lady.

For in your hands lies the hope of our salvation, and your consent will obtain our immediate release. The eternal Word of God made us, and see how we are dead men! But a word from you will see us re-made and brought back to life again.

Adam, weeping over his banishment from paradise, awaits your reply, gracious Virgin; so, too, does his unhappy posterity. Abraham and David and the rest of our holy fathers, those ancestors of yours who dwell in the land of the shadow of death — they all entreat you to give your consent. The whole world is on its knees waiting for your consent; and well it may, because upon your word hangs the hope of comfort for us wretched creatures, of our ransom from captivity, our reprieve after sentence; in a word, the hope of salvation for every child of Adam, every member of your own race.

O Mary, do be quick and let us have your answer! Make haste, and let the angel have your reply — or rather, give it to the Lord himself, with the angel for your messenger. One word from you, and the Word himself will be yours; say what you are free to say, and God will take up his abode within you. One word from you which vanishes into the air, and soon you will hold in your arms the ever-living God.

Why do you delay? What have you to fear? Believe, praise, and accept what the Lord has told you. Temper your humility with a little boldness, your feeling of inadequacy with trust. There never was a moment when virginal innocence was so urgently called upon to cast discretion to the winds. No need for you, wise Virgin, to fear presumption in a matter such as this, for though your reticence reveals a becoming modesty, your love of us requires that silence should give place to speech.

O blessed Virgin, open your heart and let faith enter in; open, too, your lips in praise and your womb to enshrine your Creator. See how he whom all the nations desire stands at the threshold of your door and knocks. What a pity if he should pass on because you are slow to open it, and you have to begin once again to seek in sorrow him whom your soul loves! Bestir yourself, and run quickly to open the door to him. Rise up, by believing what he has told you; run, by offering yourself to his service; open, by singing his praises.

And the Virgin's reply? *I am the handmaid of the Lord; let what you have said be done to me.*

DECEMBER 21

A reading from the Commentary of St Ambrose on St Luke's Gospel.
Book 2, 19, 22-23, 26-27: CCL 14, 39-42.

The Visitation of the blessed Virgin Mary

After revealing the mystery of the Incarnation, the angel told the Virgin Mary that an elderly and barren woman had conceived a child. This was to strengthen her faith and to prove, by pointing out an analogous case, that God can do whatever he wills.

On hearing this, Mary set out in haste for the hill country. Not that she doubted the angel's words or misunderstood what had been told her or questioned its truth, but rather because she was gladdened by the news, eager to serve and hastening in her joy.

Besides, where should she hasten if not to the heights, she who was now pregnant with God? The grace of the Holy Spirit admits no delay in the accomplishment of its mighty purposes; the blessings of Mary's arrival and the presence of the Lord are immediately apparent, for *as soon as Elizabeth heard Mary's greeting the child leapt in her womb and Elizabeth was filled with the Holy Spirit.*

Note the order and meaning of each word of the text: Elizabeth was the first to hear the voice but John the first to experience the grace; she heard in the natural way, he leapt for joy in a manner that is a mystery to us; she was aware of Mary's coming but he of the coming of the Lord; a woman perceived the arrival of another woman, the promised child that of another promised child; the mothers talk together about God's gift, whereas the children, who are God's gift, work within the womb and bring about a mystery of love to the benefit of their mothers; and, by a double miracle, the mothers prophecy under the influence of their little ones.

The child leapt for joy and the mother was filled with the Spirit. Not the mother before the son, but after the son was filled with the Holy Spirit he, in turn, filled his mother. John leapt for joy and the spirit of Mary rejoiced. Elizabeth was filled with the Spirit through the joy of John. As for Mary, we can see that it was not because she was filled with the Spirit that her own spirit rejoiced — something beyond our understanding was taking place in the mother in a way we cannot grasp; Elizabeth however, was filled with the Spirit *after* conceiving a child, whereas Mary was filled *before*. Elizabeth said to her: *You are blessed because you have believed.*

You also are blessed, you who have both heard and believed: for a soul that believes conceives and brings forth the Word of God and acknowledges his works. May the soul of Mary be in each one of you so that you may magnify the Lord! May the spirit of Mary be in each one of you, so that you may rejoice in God. There is but one mother of Christ according to the flesh, but Christ, through our faith, is the fruit of each one of us. For every soul receives the Divine Word within it when, free from sin or stain, it maintains its chastity undefiled.

Such a soul may well magnify the Lord, as Mary's soul magnified him, and such a spirit may well rejoice in God her Saviour. For the Lord is truly magnified, even as you have read elsewhere in Scripture: *Magnify the Lord with me;* not that anything can be added to the Lord by human utterance, but because he is magnified in us. For Christ is the Image of God, so that a soul, in doing anything excellent or devout, magnifies the Image of God in whose likeness this soul was created; and in magnifying the Image, is itself exalted by participating in the magnitude of God.

DECEMBER 22

A reading from the commentary on St Luke's Gospel by the Venerable Bede.
Lib. I, 46-55: CCL 120, 37-39.

The Magnificat

And Mary said : My soul magnifies the Lord, and my spirit exults in God my saviour. Here Mary is saying: 'The Lord has honoured me with a unique task, so sublime that words are incapable of saying what it is; even the love I bear him is of little help to my mind in trying to understand it. So I will simply go on praising and thanking him for it with all my heart. I will spend the rest of my days, I will use all my powers of thought and discernment, in contemplating the greatness of him who lives for ever. Gladly will I be the handmaid of him who is Jesus my saviour; and my spirit shall rejoice in his eternal Godhead who, in time, will be the fruit of my womb.'

For the Almighty has done great things for me, and holy is his name. We should see these words in relation to what Mary says at the beginning of her song of praise: *My soul magnifies the Lord.* Surely only she for whom the Lord had done such great things could magnify him in a way worthy of him; and invite us to join her in the praise she offers saying: *Magnify the Lord with me, and let us praise his name together.*

Here we may say that he who knows who God is and has such little esteem for him as to neglect to proclaim his greatness and to praise his holy name to the best of his ability, *he shall be considered the least in the kingdom of heaven.* We speak of his 'holy name' because such is the power and majesty of him who bears it that it places him infinitely above and apart from anything else that can be called by a name.

He has come to the help of Israel his servant, remembering his mercy. Mary expresses herself happily when she speaks of Israel as being the servant of the Lord, since it was from him that we were to receive our obedient and humble saviour. It is of him that the prophet Hosea speaks where he says: *When Israel was a child I loved him.*

If we have no regard for humility, then we are quite beyond redemption; we cannot say with the prophet: *God is my helper, and the Lord upholds my life. He, therefore, who humbles himself and becomes as a little child, he shall be the greater in the kingdom of heaven.*

According to the promise he made to our fathers, to Abraham and his sons for ever.

Mary is here talking about the spiritual, not the physical, descendants of Abraham. She means not merely those of the same line of descent, but those, whether circumcised or not, who have inherited Abraham's faith. It was before he was circumcised that Abraham believed; and it was this faith of his that was considered as having justified him.

It was for this reason, then, that the promise of a future saviour was made to Abraham and to his descendants for ever, to the children God promised him; for of them it is said: *If you belong to Christ, then you are the descendants of Abraham, his heirs according to the promise.*

Both our Lord's mother and John's mother bear eloquent prophetic witness to what was in store for us, namely that just as sin took its origin from womankind, so, too, all good things would come to us from womankind. Both mothers make it clear that though it was the deception of a woman that brought death into the world, even so, another woman would bring our Life into the world.

DECEMBER 23

A reading from the Treatise of St Hippolytus against the Heresy of Noetus.
Chapters 9-12: PG 10: 816, 817, 819.

The hidden mystery made manifest

There is one God, brethren, and only through the Holy Scriptures do we come to know him. We must therefore acquaint ourselves with everything the divine Scriptures proclaim, and accept whatever they teach. Our belief in the Father must be in accordance with his own will, and that will must also be our guide as to how we should think of the Son and understand the Holy Spirit. Let us not interpret the Holy Scriptures, which are a gift from God, according to our own pre-conceived ideas, nor distort their meaning by reliance on our own reason, but find in them what he himself wills to teach us.

When God was all alone, and nothing existed but himself, he determined to create the world. He thought of it, willed it, spoke the word, and so made it. Immediately it was with him, created according to his will. It is enough for us then to know that nothing is coeternal with God. Apart from him there was nothing in existence. Yet, though alone, he was manifold, for he was not without reason, wisdom, power or counsel. No; everything existed in him; he himself was everything. When he willed and as he willed, at the times determined by himself, he manifested his Word through whom he had made all things.

That Word which he had in himself was invisible to the created world, but God made him visible. Giving utterance to the Voice that was already within himself and engendering Light from Light, he brought forth for the world the Lord, that is, his own Mind. Formerly visible only to himself and not to the created universe, he was made visible by God, so that by his manifestation the world might be saved.

This then is the Mind that came forth into the world and was made known as the Son of God. All things came into existence through him; he alone is begotten by the Father.

God gave the law and the prophets, and by the Holy Spirit compelled those he sent to speak out. From the Father's Power they thus received the inspiration to proclaim his purpose and will.

In this way the Word was made manifest, for all that he himself had announced through the prophets is summed up by Saint John, when he shows that this was the Word through whom all things were made. Thus, *In the beginning*, he says, *there was the Word, and the Word was with God, and the Word was God. All things were made through him, and without him nothing was made.* Then further on he adds: *The world was made through him, but the world did not know him; he came to what was his own, but his own did not receive him.*

DECEMBER 24

A reading from the Sermons of St Augustine.
Sermo 185: PL 38, 997-999.

Truth has sprung up from the earth, and justice looked down from heaven

Mankind, awake! For your sake God has become man. Awake, you who sleep, and rise from the dead, and Christ will enlighten you. I tell you again, for your sake God has become man.

If he had not been born in time, you would have been dead for all eternity. If he had not assumed the likeness of sinful flesh, you would never have been freed from it. But for his mercy, you would have suffered everlasting misery; never would you have returned to life, had he not shared your death. Unless he had come to your help, you would have fallen away and perished.

And so let us joyfully celebrate the coming of our salvation and redemption, hallowing the day when he who is the great and everlasting day comes from the endless day of eternity into our own brief day of time. *He has become our justice, our holiness, our redemption, so that, as Scripture says, he who glories may glory in the Lord. Truth has sprung up from the earth* : Christ, who said *I am the Truth*, is born of a Virgin. *Justice has looked down from heaven,* for the man who believes in this new-born child is justified, not by himself, but by God. Truth has sprung up from the earth, for *the Word is made flesh;* and justice has looked down from heaven, because *every good and perfect gift comes from above.* Truth has sprung up from the earth in Mary's

66

flesh; justice has looked down from heaven, because *man can receive nothing unless it is given him by God.*

Since, then, we are justified by faith, let us have peace with God, for *justice and peace have embraced* through our Lord Jesus Christ, the Truth who has sprung up from the earth. *Through him we have access to the grace in which we stand, and our boast is in our hope of God's glory.* Not our glory, but God's, for justice has not come from us; it has looked down from heaven. *Let him who glories,* therefore, *glory in the Lord,* not in himself.

For this reason, when our Lord was born of the Virgin, angelic voices sang of *glory to God on high, and on earth peace to men of good will.* How could there be peace on earth, unless truth had sprung up from it — in other words, unless Christ were born of our human stock? *It is he who is our peace, making both one,* so that we may be men of good will, bound together in loving harmony.

Let us then rejoice in this grace, so that our glorying may be in the testimony of a good conscience, where our boasting is not in ourselves but in the Lord. This is why the Scripture says, *He is my glory, the one who lifts up my head.* For what greater grace could God have caused to dawn upon us than to make his only-begotten Son become the Son of Man, so that the sons of men in their turn might become sons of God?

Look if you will for merit, motivation, or just recompense in all this: and see whether you will find anything but sheer grace!

CHRISTMASTIDE

A reading from the Sermons of St Leo the Great.
Sermo I in Nativitate Domini, 1-3; PL 54, 190-193.

Today, dearly beloved, our Saviour is born: let us rejoice! Surely there is no place for mourning on the birthday of very Life, who has swallowed up mortality with all its fear, and brought us the joyful promise of life everlasting. No one is excluded from taking part in our jubilation. All have the same cause for gladness, for as our blessed Lord, slayer of sin and death, found none free from guilt, so has he come to set us all alike at liberty.

Let the saint exult, since he is soon to receive recompense; let the sinner give praise, since he is welcomed to forgiveness; let the pagan take courage, since he is called unto life. For in the fullness of time ordained by the inscrutable mystery of the divine decree, the Son of God clothed himself with the nature of that human race which he was to reconcile to its Maker. Thus would he vanquish the devil, the author of death, through that very nature which had once yielded him the victory.

And so at our Lord's birth the angels sing their song of joy: *Glory to God in the highest,* proclaiming *peace upon earth to men of good will;* for they see the heavenly Jerusalem being built up out of all the peoples of the world. When the angels, then, exalted as they are, find in this inexpressible act of divine love so great a cause for gladness, how much happiness should it bring to the lowly hearts of men!

Wherefore, dearly beloved, let us give thanks to God the Father, through his Son, in the Holy Spirit, who by reason of his great charity with which he has loved us, has taken pity on us; and whereas we were dead in sins, has quickened us in Christ to make us a new creation in him, a new handiwork. Let us accordingly lay aside our former way of life with all its works, and claiming our joint portion in Christ's sonship, let us renounce the deeds of corrupt nature. Recognize your dignity, O Christian, and once made a sharer in the divine nature, do not by your evil conduct return to the base servitude of the past. Keep in mind of whose head and body you are a member. Never forget that you have been plucked from the power of darkness and taken up into the light and kingdom of God. By the sacrament of baptism you have become a temple of the Holy Spirit. Do not through your depravity drive away so great a guest and put yourself once more in bondage to the devil, for the blood of Christ was the price of your redemption.

THE NIGHT OFFICE OF CHRISTMAS

Mt 1 : 18-25

A reading from a Christmas Sermon by Theodotus, Bishop of Ancyra.
Edit. Schwartz, ACO t. 3, pars 1, 157-159.

The Lord of all comes in the form of a servant

The Lord of all comes in the form of a servant; and he comes as a poor man, so that he will not frighten away those souls he seeks to capture like a huntsman. He is born in an obscure town, deliberately choosing a humble dwelling-place. His mother is a simple maiden, not a great lady. And the reason for all this lowly state is so that he may gently ensnare mankind and bring us to salvation. If he had been born amid the splendour of a rich family, unbelievers would surely have said that the face of the world had been changed by the power of wealth. If he had chosen to be born in Rome, the greatest of cities, they would have ascribed the same change to the power of her citizens.

Suppose our Lord had been the son of an emperor; they would

have pointed to the advantage of authority. Imagine his father a legislator; their cry would have been, 'See what can be brought about by the law'. But, in fact, what did he do? He chose nothing but poverty and mean surroundings, everything that was plain and ordinary and, in the eyes of most people, obscure. And this so that it could be clearly seen that the Godhead alone transformed the world. That was why he chose his mother from among the poor of a very poor country, and became poor himself.

This is the lesson of the crib. Since there was no bed, our Lord was laid in a manger. This lack of the necessities of life was the best way of proclaiming the will of God. He was laid in a manger to show that he was to be the food even of simple folk. We know, in fact, how the divine Word, the Son of God, drew to himself both rich and poor, the eloquent and the inarticulate, as he lay in the manger surrounded by poverty.

See then how poverty acted as a prophecy — how his poverty showed that he who became poor for our sake is thereby made accessible to everyone. Christ made no ostentatious display of riches, which would have made people frightened to approach him; he assumed no royal state, which would have driven men away from his presence. No, he came among ordinary men as one of themselves, offering himself freely for the salvation of all mankind.

The divine Word is set before us in human form and laid in the manger to nourish the learned and the unlearned alike. I believe that Isaiah foretold this symbolic manger when he said: *The ox knows his owner, and the ass his master's crib. But Israel has not known me, and my people have not understood.* He whose riches were the Godhead itself became poor for our sake, in order to put salvation within reach of all mankind. As St Paul said: *Though he was rich, yet for our sake he became poor, so that by his povery we might become rich.*

Who was the possessor of this wealth? In what did it consist? And how did he become poor for our sake? Who was it, tell me, who once was rich and then became poor like me? He was, to all appearances, an ordinary man, but would a man of such lowly condition, born of poor parents, ever have been rich? Who then can have been the possessor of this wealth? And what was he, before he became poor for our sake? God, as we know from Scripture, is the one who enriches his creatures. It must therefore have been God himself who became poor, assuming the poverty of one who seemed to human eyes to be no more than a man. In God are all the riches of the divine nature. He it is who became poor for our sake.

Alternative reading

A reading from the Sermons of the blessed Abbot Aelred.
Sermo 2 in Natali Domini: PL 195, 226-227.

Today a Saviour is born to us

Today the Saviour of the world is born for us : Christ the Lord, in the city of David. That city is Bethlehem. We must run there as the shepherds did when they heard these tidings, and so put into action the words we traditionally chant at this season : *They sang of God's glory, they hastened to Bethlehem.*
  And this shall be a sign for you : you will find the child wrapped in swaddling bands and lying in a manger. Now this is what I say : you must love. You fear the Lord of angels, but I say, love the tiny babe; you fear the Lord of majesty, but I say, love the infant wrapped in swaddling bands; you fear him who reigns in heaven, but I say, love him who lies in the manger. What sort of sign were the shepherds given? *You will find the child wrapped in swaddling bands and lying in a manger.* It was by

this that they were to recognize their Saviour and Lord. But is there anything great about being wrapped in swaddling bands and lying in a stable — are not other children also wrapped in swaddling bands? What kind of sign, then, can this be? Indeed it is a great one, if only we understand it rightly. Such understanding will be ours if this message of love is not restricted to our hearing, but if our hearts too are illuminated by the light which accompanied the appearance of the angels. It was to teach us that only those whose minds are spiritually enlightened can truly hear the message that the angel who first proclaimed the good tidings appeared surrounded by light.

Much can be said of this sign; but as time is passing, I shall say little, and briefly. Bethlehem, the *house of bread*, is Holy Church, in which is administered the body of Christ, the true bread. The manger at Bethlehem is the altar of the church; it is there that Christ's creatures are fed. This is the table of which it is written, *You have prepared a banquet for me*. In this manger is Jesus, wrapped in the swaddling bands which are the outward form of the sacraments. Here in this manger, under the species of bread and wine, is the true body and blood of Christ. We believe that Christ himself is here, but he is wrapped in swaddling bands; in other words, he is invisibly contained in these sacraments. We have no greater or clearer proof of Christ's birth than our daily reception of his body and blood at the holy altar, and the sight of him who was once born for us of a virgin daily offered in sacrifice for us. And so, brethren, let us hasten to the manger of the Lord. But before drawing near we must prepare ourselves as well as we can with the help of his grace; and then, in company with the angels, with pure heart, good conscience and unfeigned faith, we may sing to the Lord in all that we do throughout the whole of our life: *Glory to God in the highest, and peace on earth to men of good will;* through our Lord Jesus Christ, to whom be honour and glory for ever and ever. Amen.

Alternative reading

A reading from a Homily of Saint Basil the Great.
Hom in sanctam Christi generationem 2, 6; PG 31, 1459-1462, 1471-1474.

The Word was made flesh, and dwelt among us

Once more God has come to our world, and is found among men. Not as the divine Lawgiver does he come to us now, with flashes of lightning and loud trumpet blast, to a mountain wreathed in smoke, dense cloud and stormy winds, striking terror into the hearts of the hearers. His coming is as a man of flesh and blood who gently enters into familiar converse with us, after the human fashion of those whose nature he shares. Now God is in our human existence, no longer working intermittently through the prophets. He has taken humanity to himself and made himself one with it. Through his kinship with our condition he has raised the whole of mankind to his own.

Yet how, we may ask, can glory come to all through one man alone? In what way can flesh contain the Godhead? In the way that fire is present in iron; not by one substance giving way to the other, but by one imparting some further quality to the other. The fire does not, as it were, rush towards the iron; it gives its own strength to the iron while remaining in its own place. And this participation does not in any way diminish the fire, for it completely fills whatever shares in its substance. So in the same way God the Word did not relinquish his own Person when, as the Scripture says, *He dwelt among us;* nor did he suffer any change when *the Word was made flesh.* Heaven was not left forsaken of him who holds all things together, but earth received in its midst the one who dwells in eternal blessedness.

Let us try to fathom this mystery. By coming in the flesh, God has won a decisive victory over death which was lurking in the flesh. Just as disease is overcome by the curative properties of medicines adapted to the body's needs, and as the darkness in a house is dispelled by the approach of light, so in the same way that death which held sway over our human nature was abolished at the coming of the Godhead. To take a further example : as long as night and darkness last, the ice which has formed in water will cover its surface, but under the warmth of the sun it will gradually melt. So it was that until the advent of Christ, death was master; but when the loving kindness of God our Saviour appeared and the Sun of Justice rose, death was swallowed up in victory, unable to endure the presence of the true life. How deep is the goodness of God; how far-reaching his love for mankind!

With the shepherds let us rejoice, joining in the angels' song : *For to us is born this day a Saviour who is Christ the Lord.* The Lord God is our light. He would not appear to us in the form of God, let he should startle the weak; rather he comes in the form of a servant in order to set free what was captive. Who is so dull of heart, so ungracious, that he will not rejoice, be glad and exult with all who are present? This is a feast in which the whole of creation shares. Let no one come empty-handed, none without gratitude; and may we, too, lift up our voices in a song of joy.

Sunday within the Octave of Christmas

A reading from the Allocutions of Pope Paul VI
(Nazareth, 5 January 1964)

The Example of Nazareth

The home at Nazareth is the school in which the life of Christ begins to take shape : it is the school of the Gospel. Here we first learn to look, to listen, to meditate, to gain a thorough understanding of the deep and secret power that underlies this very simple, humble and beautiful revelation of God's Son; here we may perhaps learn, by degrees, to imitate.

Here too we begin to learn the way in which we may reach a simple understanding of who Christ is. Here above all we realize how continually we must meditate upon every detail of his life among us — the scenes, occasions, customs, words, religious observances — everything in fact that Jesus used in order to reveal himself to the world. Everything here tells us something, everything here has meaning.

Here assuredly, in this school, we learn to appreciate the need for a man to maintain a spiritual discipline if he wishes to follow the teaching of the Gospel and be a disciple of Christ. If the wish could be granted, how gladly should we return to our childhood and go to school again here in Nazareth, to a school at once humble and sublime! How eager we should be to return to our studies and to learn at Mary's side a true understanding of life and to set our minds on the truths of God!

It is really, however, only as pilgrims that we visit Nazareth, and we must set aside the wish to stay here in order to deepen our knowledge of the Gospel. Let us not leave, though, without quickly taking hold of some brief gleanings of wisdom from this home in Nazareth, to remind us of it.

The first thing this home teaches us is silence. If only we could once again value it at its true worth, silence, that singular and totally necessary habit of mind, when we are assailed by so much shouting, bustle and noise in this feverish age of ours in conditions of such continual stress. May the silence of Nazareth teach us to keep our minds fixed on holy things, our souls directed towards the interior life of the spirit, ready to hear the secret counsels of God and the guidance of experienced spiritual masters. May it teach us how essential and valuable are the preliminaries: study, meditation, a personal and searching rule of life, and the prayer that God alone sees in secret.

It is here again that we discover the pattern of family life. Let Nazareth remind us of what the family really is, with its fellowship of love, its profound and radiant beauty, its holy and inviolable unity; let it show how good the life of a family is, which nothing else can replace; let it teach us the true role of the family in society.

Finally, it is here that we learn the discipline of work. In this house at Nazareth, home of the carpenter's Son, we desire above all to learn and to proclaim the strength and freedom given by man's work, to pay tribute here to the dignity of labour so that everyone may experience it; under this roof we would remind you of the truth that work cannot be an end in itself, but takes its freedom and its excellence not so much from what is called its economic value as from those things that direct it towards its true goal. Finally, in this house we would proclaim salvation to all who labour throughout the world, setting before them a great model, their divine brother, their spokesman in all just causes that concern them: Christ, our Lord.

A reading from a Homily of St John Chrysostom on the Day of Our Lord's Birth.
PG 56, 392.

Mary and Joseph with the Child Jesus

Today the Firstborn of the Virgin goes down into Egypt, to put an end to the mourning which has lain upon the land since the destruction of its firstborn sons. His coming brings joy where there were plagues, and the light of salvation where night and darkness formerly reigned.

In days of old the river water had been polluted by the slaughter of innocent children. Now the Lord, who turned it into blood, himself visits Egypt. By the might of his Holy Spirit he cleanses its streams of defilement and endows them with the power to bring forth salvation. When God afflicted the Egyptians and chastised them in his anger, they rejected him. Now, therefore, the Lord enters their country and, by filling devout men with the knowledge of God, causes its waters to nurture martyrs more numerous than the reeds of the river.

The divine Word, while remaining for ever immutable, has become man. What more shall I say of this mystery? Before my eyes are a workman and a crib, an infant and swaddling bands, a virgin in childbirth lacking even the necessities of life — everything in utter deprivation, an abundance only of poverty. Were riches ever seen in such total want? See how he who has so much has made himself poor for our sake, possessing neither bed nor cover, but lying like an outcast in a bare manger! Here, poverty is the source of all riches. Here, plenty is concealed in destitution. He lies in a manger, and the foundations of the world are shaken. Wrapped in swaddling bands, he bursts the bonds of sin. Before he has begun to speak he teaches the wise men and changes their hearts. What more is there to say? Here is the Child, wrapped in swaddling bands. With him is Mary, virgin and mother; here too is Joseph, who is called his father.

Joseph was betrothed to Mary, no more, when the Holy Spirit overshadowed her. Hence he was sorely perplexed, not knowing what name the Child should bear. In his anxiety, an angel's voice brought him reassurance from heaven: 'Joseph, do not fear, for what has been conceived in her is of the Holy Spirit; in her virginity the Spirit has overshadowed her.'

We may ask why the child should be born of a virgin, why her maidenhood should be preserved inviolate. The answer must be that the devil, long before, had deceived the virgin Eve; and so the angel Gabriel brought his glad tidings to another virgin, Mary. Caught in the snare, Eve uttered a word that brought death in its wake. But when Mary received the good news, she gave birth to the incarnate Word, who has given us eternal life.

YEAR 2. Lk 2 : 22-40 or 2 : 39-40

A reading from a Homily by the Venerable Bede.
Hom 1, 19: CCL 122, 134-135, 138-139.

Jesus increased in wisdom, and in stature, and in grace

Beloved brethren, the meaning of the gospel that has just been read is clear, and we do not need to discuss what there is to expound in it. It describes the infancy and boyhood of our Redeemer, in which he deigned to become a sharer in our humanity; it recalls the timelessness of the divine majesty, in which he remained, and always will remain, equal to the Father. Clearly this is so that we, having in mind the humility of his incarnation, should set ourselves to learn from it true humility, the cure for the wounds of all sins. We who are dust and ashes should meditate with faithful hearts on how much we ought to humble ourselves, both out of love for God and for our own salvation, when he who is the ultimate power did not disdain to be humbled for us, taking upon himself the imperfection of our frailty.

The fact that at twelve years old he sat in the Temple among the doctors, listening and asking questions, is a sign or rather an outstanding example of the humility that we must learn. The fact that as he sat in the Temple the Lord said: *I must be about my Father's business*, proclaims that his power and glory is co-eternal with that of God his Father. But the fact that he returned to Nazareth and was under the authority of his parents is at once a sign of his true humanity and an example of humility. For it was in his human nature, in which he was less than the Father, that he was subject to human authority.

And his Mother kept all these things, pondering them in her heart. Everything that she knew to have been said or done by the Lord or concerning him the Virgin Mother kept diligently in her heart. She committed it all carefully to memory, so that when the time should come for preaching or writing about the Lord's incarnation she could base her explanations to enquirers upon a complete record of his deeds.

Let us too, my brethren, imitate the faithful Mother of the Lord, and repel the invasion of vain and harmful thoughts by imprinting on our hearts every word and deed of our Lord and Saviour and meditating on them day and night. For if we wish in the blessed age to come to dwell in the house of the Lord and to praise him for ever, we must anticipate in this age, by our frequent visits to the church, what we seek in the age to come; and this not only by singing God's praises in church, but by showing forth in every place where he rules, both in words and in deeds, those things that redound to the praise and glory of our Creator.

It is good that after it has been said that *Jesus increased in wisdom and in stature and in favour* there is added *with God and men.* Because as by growing in stature he made accessible to men the gifts of wisdom and grace that were his; so likewise he tirelessly roused them to the praise of God the Father, carrying out himself what he taught others to do: *Let your light so shine before men that they may see your good works and give glory to your Father in heaven.*

YEAR 3. Lk 2 : 41-52

A reading from Origen's Homilies on the Gospel of St Luke. Hom 18, 2-5; GCS 9, 112-113.

Seeking Jesus anxiously

When he was twelve years old, the boy Jesus stayed behind in Jerusalem. Not knowing this, his parents sought him anxiously, but did not find him. Though they searched the whole caravan, looking for him among their kinsfolk and acquaintances, he was nowhere to be found. It was his own parents who were looking for him — the father who had brought him up and cared for him when they fled into Egypt — and even they did not find him at once. This shows that Jesus is not found among relatives and acquaintances, not among those bound to him by physical ties. We do not find him in a crowd. Let us learn where it was that Joseph and Mary discovered him, then in their company we too shall be able to find him. They found him, scripture says, in the temple. Not just anywhere, but in the temple; and not just anywhere in the temple, but among the doctors, listening to them and asking them questions. And so we too must look for Jesus in the temple of God; we must look for him in the Church, among the doctors who belong to the Church and do not depart from her teaching. If we seek in this way, we shall find him. Moreover, if anyone claims to be a doctor without possessing Christ, he is a doctor in name only; Jesus, the Word and Wisdom of God, will not be found with him. They found him, then, *sitting among the doctors*, or rather not merely sitting, but learning from them and listening to them.

At this very moment Jesus is present among us too, questioning us and listening to us speaking.

It is further written, *And they were all amazed*. What caused their astonishment? Not his questions — though these were certainly extraordinary — but his answers. He questioned the doctors, and since they could not always give an answer, he himself replied to his own questions. These replies were not mere disputation, but real teaching, exemplified for us in holy scripture where the divine law declares: *Moses spoke, and God answered him*.

In this way the Lord instructed Moses about those matters of which he was ignorant. So it was that sometimes Jesus asked questions, sometimes he answered them; and, as we have already said, wonderful though his questions were, his replies were even more wonderful. In order, therefore, that we too may be his hearers and that he may put to us questions which he himself will then answer, let us pray to him earnestly, seeking him with great effort and anguish, and then our search will be rewarded. Not for nothing was it written: *Your father and I have been looking for you anxiously*. The search for Jesus must be neither careless nor indifferent, nor must it be only a transitory affair. Those who seek in this manner will never find him. We must truly be able to say: *We have been looking for you anxiously*; if we can say this, then he will reply to our weary and anxious soul in the words: *Did you not know that I must be in my Father's house?*

DECEMBER 29

A reading from the Sermons of St Bernard.
On the Epiphany of the Lord, Sermon 1, 1. 2: PL 133, 141-143.

When the fulness of time had come, then came also the fulness of the Godhead

The goodness and humanity of God our Saviour have appeared : let us give thanks to God for such a great consolation in this unhappy life of wandering and exile. Before the humanity of God appeared, his goodness was concealed. Even then he was good of course, for the mercy of the Lord is eternal, but how could we have known that? People had no faith in promises which their own experience did not confirm. *The Lord had spoken through the prophets in many different ways. I think thoughts of peace, and not of affliction* he had assured us. But what did man reply — man who knew no peace but was all too conscious of his afflictions? How long will you go on saying, *Peace, peace, when there is no peace?* Then *the messengers of peace wept bitterly* and said: *Lord, who has believed in our words?* But at last God has given evidence of the most convincing kind, for men do at least believe their own eyes. He does not wish to be hidden from those troubled eyes, so *he has placed his dwelling in the sun.*

Now what do we see? Peace not only promised but sent; not only announced but given; not only prophesied but made present. An apt comparison would be a bulging purse which God the Father in his mercy sent down from heaven; a purse moreover that was torn open in the Passion to pour out everything it held — the price of our redemption. It was only a small purse, but it was very full. *For unto us a child is given :* a child, yes; but one *in whom dwells all the fulness of the Godhead.*

For when the fulness of time had come, then came also the fulness of the Godhead. God himself came in a human body, because only in this way could he show himself to men of flesh and blood, and, by the sight of his humanity, convince us of his goodness. Knowing that humanity would put his goodness beyond all question, for what means could possibly have been more effective in persuading me of that goodness than his taking to himself my human nature? My human nature, I say, not Adam's — at least not Adam's as it was before he sinned.

What more clearly manifests his mercy than his assumption of my misery? What better demonstrates the depths of his compassion than the fact that for my sake he, the Word of God, became as grass. *O Lord, what is man that you should be mindful of him? Why should you set your heart on him?* Surely this ought to make us stop and think how much God cares for us, and teach us how God thinks of us and feels for us. We must not draw conclusions from our own sufferings, but must remember his. We must learn from what he became for us how highly he has exalted us : then his humanity will be a revelation of his goodness. In fact, the depths of his humiliation in assuming that humanity is our proof of the depths of his love : the more vile he became on account of me, so much the more did he show his love for me. *The goodness and humanity of God our Saviour have appeared,* announced the Apostle. Truly great is the goodness of God, and manifest his humanity. Indeed he has given us the most positive proof of his goodness by the pains he took to enrich our humanity with his own divine dignity.

DECEMBER 30

A reading from 'The Refutation of all Heresies' by St Hippolytus. 16. 33-34: PG 3451. 3454.

We are made sharers in the Godhead by the Word made flesh

Our faith does not rest upon empty words; we are not carried away by mere caprice nor taken in by specious arguments, but neither do we turn a deaf ear when a message comes from the Power of God. Such a message God entrusted to his Word, who delivered it to mankind in order to cure us of our disobedience, not by forcibly reducing us to slavery, but by addressing to our free will a call to liberty.

In these last days the Father sent the Word in person, for he no longer wished it to be spoken by prophets and proclaimed in such an obscure way as to be only dimly apprehended. He instructed the Word to show himself openly so that by the actual sight of him the world might be won over. We know the story: how he took for himself a body from the Virgin and so re-fashioned our fallen nature. We know that his manhood was of the same clay as our own, because otherwise any precepts about following our teacher's example would have been given in vain. If he were made of a different substance from me, how could he expect me to imitate him when by my very nature I am so weak? How could such a demand be reconciled with his goodness and justice?

No; he wanted us to realize that he was like ourselves, and so he worked hard, he experienced hunger and thirst, he slept. Without protest he endured his passion, submitted to death, and then showed himself risen from the grave. In all of these acts he offered his own manhood as first-fruits, to keep us from losing heart when suffering comes our way, and make us look forward to receiving the same reward as he did, possessed as we are of the same humanity.

Then, when we have come to know God as he is, our bodies will be immortal and incorruptible like our souls. We who have paid homage to the heavenly King during our life on earth will receive the Kingdom of Heaven. Friends of God and co-heirs with Christ, we shall no longer be subject to desire, passion or disease, for we shall share in the divine nature. God, by the very fact that he made us men, subjected us to suffering; but when we have been made sharers in his Godhead, and immortal, he has promised us that his attributes will be ours. This explains the saying: 'Know yourself', and so learn to know the God who made you in his own image, for when a man is called by God, it is to know him and be known by him.

It is not for us men therefore to be at enmity with one another, but to change our way of life without delay. For Christ, who is God, exalted above all creation, has determined by washing away man's sin to renew our fallen nature, which from the beginning he had called his image. In this decision of his he gave proof of his love for us. If we obey his holy commandments, and by our own goodness imitate him who is good, he will honour us by making us like himself. God does not lack means, and for the sake of his own glory he will even admit us to a share in his divinity.

DECEMBER 31

A reading from the Sermons of St Leo the Great.
Sermo VI in Nativitate Domini, 2-3, 5; PL 54, 213-216.

Our Lord's birthday is the birthday of peace

Although with the years that childhood which the Son of God had not found unworthy of his majesty matured to manhood, and those lowly actions which he had embraced on our account came to an end with his victorious passion and resurrection, it still remains true that for us the Nativity of Jesus, Son of the Virgin Mary, is a renewal of the sacred beginnings of his life on earth, and that in celebrating our Saviour's birthday we find ourselves celebrating our own. For the birth of Christ is the fountain-head of the whole Christian people; the birthday of head and body are one and the same. Each of us is called in his turn, and the children of the Church are separated from one another by intervals of time. Yet just as the whole body of the faithful was crucified with Christ at the time of his passion, rose with him at Easter and ascended with him to the Father's right hand, so too all who have been re-born in the baptismal font were born with him on this day. Whatever part of the world a believer may live in, when he is born again in Christ he breaks with his former way of life and becomes a new man. His earthly lineage now counts for nothing; he belongs to the family of our Saviour, who became the Son of Man so that we might become the sons of God. Unless Christ had so lowered himself to come down to us, no merit of our own could have enabled us to reach him.

Hence the very greatness of the gift bestowed on us demands a reverence worthy of its excellence. As the blessed apostle teacher us, *we have not received the spirit of this world, but* the Spirit which is of God, in order that we may know what gifts God has given us. The only way we can pay him fitting honour is to offer him his own gifts. And in the treasury of his bounty what could we find more appropriate to this feast than that peace which was first proclaimed by the angel choir at our Lord's nativity? It is peace which gives birth to the children of God, which fosters love and is the mother of unity; it is the rest of the blessed and the dwelling place of eternity. Its proper work and special grace is to detach men from the world and unite them to God.

Let those who are born not of blood, nor of the desire of the flesh, nor of the will of man, but of God, offer to their Father the harmony of sons at peace with one another, and let all his adopted members meet in the Firstborn of the new creation, who came not to do his own will but the will of him who sent him. It is surely not those who are at variance and have nothing in common whom the Father has graciously adopted as his heirs, but those who love each other and share the same sentiments. Re-fashioned after a single pattern, they ought to be one in mind. Our Lord's birthday is the birthday of peace. This is the teaching of the apostle: He is our peace, who has made us both one; for whether we are Jews or Gentiles, we have access through him in one Spirit to the Father.

A reading from the Letter of St Athanasius to Epictetus.
Ep. ad Epict. 5-9; PG 26: 1057, 1061-1065.

The Word of God received our human nature from Mary

The divine Word took lineal descent from Abraham, as the
apostle tells us, *for in order to resemble his brothers in every
way, it was necessary for him to possess a body like ours.* Consequently, Mary's role in the Incarnation was fundamental,
because from her Christ received as his own the body which he
offered in sacrifice for us. The Scriptures therefore contain the
record of Mary's child-bearing, describing how she wrapped her
son in swaddling clothes; they tell us of the blessing called down
upon the breasts that nursed him, and of the sacrifice that was
offered, as for a first-born son. Gabriel's message to Mary had
been carefully worded. He did not say simply, 'what will be born
in you', for then men might think that the child's body had
gained entrance to her womb from without. What he said was,
'*from* you', to convince them that her son was brought forth
naturally from her own body.

So it was that the Word took to himself what was ours and
offered it in sacrifice, in order to destroy its infirmities and clothe
us in what was his, thus inspiring St Paul to write, *What is
corruptible must put on incorruption, and what is mortal must
put on immortality.*

These things were no mere pretence, as some have supposed;
God preserve us from such an error. It was only because our
Saviour became a real man that the whole man was saved. No
indeed, this salvation of ours is no empty appearance, nor does
it end with our bodies. The whole man, body and soul, has
truly been saved in the Word of God himself.

According to the Scriptures, then, Mary's son was man by nature, and the Lord's body was a real one; real, because the same as our own. For Mary is our sister, since all of us are children of Adam.

When St John says *The Word was made flesh*, this does not mean that he was changed into a man, but that he assumed our human nature. St Paul uses a similar expression when he writes *Christ was made a curse for our sakes*. However, from its union and close fellowship with the Word, the human body has gained tremendous dignity. Mortal before, it has now become immortal; carnal before, it has become spiritual; a creature of earth, it has entered the gates of heaven.

Nevertheless, even though the Word took a body from Mary, the Trinity is still a trinity. Nothing can be added to it, nothing taken away; it remains eternally perfect. In its three Persons we acknowledge one divine Nature, and thus the Church proclaims: There is one God, the Father of the Word.

Lk 2 : 16-21

A reading from the Sermons of St Cyril of Alexandria.
Sermon 15, 1-3: On the Incarnation of the Word of God. PG 77, 1089, 1091.

The holy Virgin is to be given the title 'Mother of God'

Deep, momentous and truly marvellous is the mystery of our faith, eagerly awaited by the holy angels themselves. As the Lord's disciple declares when he refers to what the holy prophets had said of Christ, the Saviour of the world: *the angels long for insight into the things which the preachers of the Good News, in the power of the Holy Spirit sent from heaven, have now revealed to you.* And when Christ was born as one of human kind, all those angels whose gaze penetrated and grasped the tremendous mystery of our faith gave thanks on our behalf: *Glory to God in the highest,* they sang, *and on earth peace, good will among men.*

For Christ was by nature true God. He was the Word of God the Father, with whom he was one in substance and co-eternal, and at the same time resplendent in his own sublime majesty. Yet although he shared the nature of the One who begot him and was his equal, *he did not count his equality with God as something to be clung to, but divested himself of his dignity, and taking* from holy Mary *the nature of a slave was born a man, and in that human condition humbled himself even to the extent of dying, dying on a cross.* Thus he who gives to all things of his plenitude lowered himself of his own free will for our sake. Being under no constraint, he who by his own nature was free, chose for our sake to take the nature of a slave. He who is exalted above every creature became one of us. He who *is the living bread that gives life to the world* became one of those destined to die; he who, as God, is lawgiver and above every law became subject to the law as we are. He who existed before all ages, before time, or rather, who was himself their creator, became one of those who must be born, must have a beginning.

How did he become like us? By taking from the holy Virgin a body, and one endowed with a rational soul so that he came forth from the woman as a true man, but without sin. Yet man though he was in all reality and not merely in outward appearance, he did not lay aside his divinity and cease to be God as he had always been and is and ever will be. We therefore call the Holy Virgin by the title: Mother of God.

A reading from Origen's Treatise 'Concerning First Principles'.
Book 2, Chapter 6, 1-2: On the Incarnation of Christ.

The mystery of Christ must be contemplated with
profound awe and reverence

Reflecting on the statements of Holy Scripture that tell of his majesty who is Lord of all creation, we marvel that he is called the *image of the invisible God, the first-born of all creation; that in him everything visible and invisible was created, the whole universe was created through him and for him;* and *that he is before all things, and in him all things hold together* — yet faced by the glory of the Saviour, how pale are any words!

When we ponder these tremendous truths concerning the Son of God, we are struck with profound amazement that he whose nature was sublime beyond compare stripped himself of his state of majesty, became a man, and lived among men.

Before appearing himself in a human body he had sent prophets, forerunners and heralds of his coming. Moreover, after his ascension into heaven he caused his holy Apostles, simple, unlearned men from the ranks of tax-collectors and fishermen, whom he filled with his divine power, to travel over the whole world and gather together out of every race and nation a devoted multitude of believers. But what more than all his other mighty and marvellous works overwhelms the human mind with wonder and dumbfounds mortal man's poor understanding is that the mighty Power of divine Majesty, the very Word of the Father, the very Wisdom of God in whom everything visible and invisible was created, was confined, as we believe, within a man who appeared in Judaea; that the Wisdom of God entered the womb of a woman, was born a baby, and

93

cried like a baby, and that later this same Wisdom of God was deeply troubled as a man at the prospect of death, as was related of him and as he also acknowledges himself when he says: *My soul is sorrowful, even unto death;* and that he was brought at the last to what is in the eyes of men the most shameful of deaths, although he rose again on the third day.

When we thus see in him some features so human as to appear no different from the frailty common to all mortals, and others so divine that they befit none but the primal and ineffable nature of the Godhead, the feeble human intellect is baffled, stupefied with such amazement that it sees no means of penetrating the paradox, does not know what to hold on to, which way to turn. If it thinks of God, it sees a mortal; if it thinks of a man, it sees the empire of death overthrown, and this man returning from the grave with its spoils. It is with the most profound awe and reverence therefore that we must contemplate this mystery.

JANUARY 2

A reading from the Treatise on the Holy Spirit by St Basil the Great.
26, 61. 64: SC 466. 468. 470. 474. 476.

The Lord gives life to his body through the Spirit

What do we mean when we speak of someone being a very spiritual person? Simply that he is led by the Spirit of God, is called a son of God, and is taking on a likeness to the Son of God. No longer does he live by the standards of the world. It is something like the faculty of sight which exists in a healthy eye, for a purified soul has within it the action of the Spirit. A man's word is another example. It may be either a thought contained within his heart or syllables pronounced by his tongue, and it is the same with the Holy Spirit. There are times when it bears witness to our spirit, crying out in our hearts, 'Abba, Father', and others when it speaks in our stead, as Scripture says, *You are not the one who is speaking : it is the Spirit of God that is speaking in you.*

We may also think of the Spirit in another way; namely, as a whole present in all its parts in accordance with the distribution of God's gifts. For we are all members of one another, even though, by the grace of God, we have different endowments. This is why *the eye cannot say to the hand, 'I can manage without you', nor the head to the feet, 'I do not need you'.* On the contrary, all the members together make up the body of Christ, in the unity of the Spirit, and each uses the special ability given it to serve the others according to their need. For although God has disposed the various parts of the body as he has seen fit, there exists among them all a spiritual fellowship that makes it natural for them to share one another's feelings, and be concerned for one another. *So it is that when one member suffers, all the members suffer with it; when one member is honoured, all the members rejoice with it.* Moreover, as parts exist in the whole, so each of us is in the Spirit, for all who belong to the one Body have been baptized into the one Spirit.

Now as the Father is seen in the Son, so likewise is the Son seen in the Spirit. To worship in the Spirit, therefore, is to open one's mind to the divine Light. We can learn all this from our Lord's words to the woman of Samaria. Deceived by local custom, she believed it was necessary to worship in a certain place, but correcting her, our Lord declared that it was in Spirit and in Truth that one must worship, and by Truth he clearly meant himself.

Accordingly, when we speak of adoration in the Son, we mean that we worship God as he is revealed in the Son, who is the image of God; and similarly, saying that we adore in the Spirit means that we worship the Lord whose divinity is revealed by the Spirit. Thus the Spirit enlightens us to perceive the Son, who is the radiance of the glory of God; and the Son, who bears the very stamp of the Father, then raises us up to the Father, to whom belong both the Stamp, and its Seal of identical form, which is the Holy Spirit.

JANUARY 3

A reading from St Augustine's Commentary on John.
Tract. 17, 7-9: CCL 36, 174-175.

The twin commandments of charity

The Lord has come in the fullness of his love, to teach us how to love. In his own person, as was prophesied of him, he sums up the whole of God's message to the world, and shows that all the Law and the Prophets hang upon the twin commandments of charity.

Now, brethren, call to mind with me what these two commandments are. They ought, indeed, to be most familiar to you, not something that only recurs to your thoughts when I jog your memory, for they should never be erased from your hearts. Always and above all things remember that you must love God and your neighbour. *You must love God with all your heart and with all your soul and with all your mind; and you must love your neighbour as yourself.* Think on these things at all times; dwell on them, hold on to them, act on them, fulfil them. Love of God is the first to be enjoined, but love of neighbour is the first to be observed, for in giving a two-fold commandment of love, our Lord would not put neighbour before God. No; God first, then neighbour. But since you cannot yet see God, you have the assurance that by loving your neighbour you will come to the sight of him. Love of neighbour cleanses your eyes and makes them capable of seeing God. St John tells us this plainly : *If you do not love the brother you can see*, he says, *how will you be able to love the God you cannot see?*

Here, then, are your orders: you are to love God. Show him to me, you may say, so that I can love him. My only answer is to say with St John : *No man has ever seen God.* But St John does not mean you to think yourself altogether excluded from the vision of God, for he says: *God is love, and anyone who lives in love lives in God.* Love your neighbour, then. Look within yourself for the power to love him, and there, as far as you may, you will see God.

Begin, therefore, to love your neighbour. *Break your bread for the hungry, and bring the homeless and needy into your house. If you see a man naked, clothe him, and do not turn from your own kin.* What will your reward be for these things? *Your light will break forth like the dawn.* Your light is your God. He is the dawn coming to you after the night of this world, the morning star that neither rises nor sets, but endures for ever.

By loving and caring for your neighbour you advance on your journey — the journey whose one goal is the Lord our God, whom we are bound to love with all our heart and all our soul and all our mind. We have not yet come into the Lord's presence, but our neighbour is with us here and now. As you travel with him, then, be his support, so that you may reach your goal: the Lord with whom you desire to dwell for ever.

JANUARY 4

A reading from the Five Hundred Chapters of St Maximus the Confessor.
Centuria 1, 8-13; PG 90, 1182-1186.

A mystery that is always new

The Word of God, born once for all according to the flesh, is pleased to be born anew at every instant, according to the spirit, to all those who desire him, for he delights in the qualities of goodness and humanity. He becomes a little child, clothing himself in those same qualities and revealing himself in such dimensions as he knows they can accept. It is not from any trace of ill-will or aversion that he thus diminishes the manifestation of his true greatness; he is but taking the measure of the capacity of those who long to see him. Hence the Word of God, while revealing himself in modes suited to those with whom he holds communion, remains — and this is where the mystery is so overwhelmingly great — for ever inaccessible to the sight of all.

That is why the divine Apostle, with a wise insight into the meaning of the mystery, exclaims: *Jesus Christ, yesterday and today, the same for ever.* For he truly perceives that the mystery is always new and that it never grows old in the mind's understanding.

Christ our God is born. He who himself created all things out of nothing takes flesh endowed with a human soul and is made man. A star from the east, visible during the day, guides the Magi to the place where the Word made flesh is lying, in order to show that the Word, which is the main object of the Law and the Prophets, mysteriously confounds the evidence of the senses and guides the nations towards the fullest light of understanding.

For clearly, when understood in a spirit of reverence, the language of the Law and the Prophets may be compared to a star leading those who have been called by the power of grace to recognize the incarnate Word.

God therefore becomes perfect man, changing nothing of man's nature except sin, which was in the beginning not part of his nature. Using his own body as bait, he tempts the insatiable dragon, waiting with gaping jaws to devour him, into making an assault upon this flesh that will prove his undoing. By the power of the godhead within it, this flesh will bring the devil to utter destruction; whereas for human nature this same flesh will be the sovereign remedy, restoring man to the grace that was his from the beginning through the power of the godhead within his very flesh. For as the serpent, by infusing the poison of wickedness into the tree of knowledge, destroyed the nature that tasted it, so he himself, in his eagerness to devour the Master's flesh, was destroyed by the power of the godhead within it.

The great mystery of the divine Incarnation remains a mystery for ever. How can the Word truly and substantially exist in the flesh, while at the same time his whole being is with the Father? How can that same Word, who is wholly divine by nature, have become completely human without in any way disowning either his divine nature in which he subsists as God, or ours in which he was made man?

Faith alone is able to perceive these mysteries, which themselves are truly the essence and the foundation of those things that surpass what the mind can either see or understand.

JANUARY 5

A reading from the Sermons of St Augustine.
Sermo 194, 3-4; PL 38: 1016-1017.

The sight of your Word will fulfil all our longing

What man is there who knows all the treasures of wisdom and knowledge hidden in Christ and concealed in the poverty of his human condition? *Rich though he was, he became poor on our account, so that through his poverty we might become rich.* When he assumed our mortality and destroyed our death, he appeared among us as a poor man; not because anyone had robbed him of his wealth, but because he was keeping his promised riches in reserve.

How great is the goodness that he holds in store for those who fear him, and shows to those who trust him! We know it only in part; the fullness is yet to come. It was to make us capable of receiving it in its entirety that he, who in his divine nature is equal to the Father, took the nature of a slave. He assumed our likeness in order to re-model us in the likeness of God. When God's only Son became the Son of Man, he made many sons of men become the sons of God. Having schooled them by his appearance in their own servile condition, he gave them their freedom and the capacity to see him in his divine nature.

For we are now the sons of God; what we are to be in the future has not yet been revealed. We only know that when this revelation does take place we shall reflect God's likeness, because we shall see him as he is. How, indeed, could those treasures of wisdom and knowledge, that divine wealth, be insufficient for us? How could that abundant goodness fail to satisfy us? *Show us,* then, *the Father, and it will be enough for us.*

One of our own race, speaking both in us and for us, says to the Lord in the psalms: *My desire will be fulfilled when your glory is revealed.* But since he and the Father are one, he who sees him sees the Father also. *The Lord of hosts,* therefore, *is the King of glory.* He will bring us back, his face will shine on us, and then we shall be saved; we shall have our fill, and he will be enough for us.

Until all this is accomplished and he gives us the vision that will satisfy us; until we are able to drink deep at the fountain of life of which he is the source; while we are still absent from him, walking by faith, hungry and thirsty for righteousness and consumed with longing to see the beauty of his godhead; let us now humbly and devoutly celebrate his birth in servant's estate.

Though we can as yet form no idea of his generation from the Father before the break of day, let us dwell in thought upon his birth from the Virgin during the hours of night. His name, as old as the sun, is still beyond our understanding; but at least we may discern the dwelling place he has made for himself beneath the sun. If we cannot yet behold him as the only Son abiding with the Father, let us ponder on his coming forth like a bridegroom from his tent; and although we are not worthy to take a seat at the table of our heavenly Father, let us recognize our place before the manger of our Lord Jesus Christ.

A reading from the Sermons of Pope St Leo the Great.
Sermo 3 in Epiphania Domini, 1-3, 5; PL 54, 240-244.

*God has made known his salvation
throughout the whole world*

Seeing the world on the way to perdition, and determining to rescue it in these latter days by his merciful providence, God fore-ordained the salvation of all peoples in Christ. These peoples constitute that numberless offspring which was promised of old to the blessed patriarch Abraham, an offspring he would acquire not according to the laws of nature but according to the fecundity of faith. Told that his descendants would be countless as the stars, the father of all nations was given the hope of a posterity that would be not of the earth, but of heaven.

Let the full number of the nations, then, take their place in the family of the patriarchs; let the gentiles enter, and the sons of the promise receive the blessing of Abraham's race which was rejected by his own flesh and blood. In the persons of the three Wise Men, let all peoples worship the Creator of the universe, and God be known no longer in Judea alone, but throughout the whole world, so that in every place *in Israel his name may be magnified.*

Therefore, dearly beloved, since we have been instructed in the mysteries of divine grace, let us celebrate the day of our first fruits and the initial call of the gentiles with spiritual joy and gratitude to the God of all mercies, *who has qualified us,* in the words of the apostle, *to share the lot of the saints in light, and has delivered us from the power of darkness, transferring us to the kingdom of his beloved Son.* According to the prophecy of Isaiah, *the people who sat in darkness have seen a great light, and day has dawned upon those who dwelt in the shadow of death.* In the same vein the prophet addressed the Lord, saying: *Nations to whom you were unknown will call upon your name, and people who never knew you will fly to you for refuge.*

Abraham saw this day, and rejoiced to know that in his off-spring, that is in Christ, the children of his faith were to be blessed, and that by believing he was to become the father of all nations. *He gave glory to God, in the firm conviction that he was able to fulfil what he had promised.*

This is the day of which David sang in the psalms: *All the nations you have made will come and adore you, Lord, and give glory to your name.* And again: *The Lord has made known his salvation; he has displayed his holiness in the sight of all the peoples.*

All this we know has come to pass since the three Wise Men were called from their far-off land and led by the guiding star to recognize and worship the King of heaven and earth. Surely the leadership of this star draws us also to imitate the Magi's act of homage, and to respond with all our hearts to the grace inviting every man to follow Christ. In this effort, dearly beloved, you must all help one another; then you will shine like the children of light in the kingdom of God, to which we gain admittance by sound faith and good works: through our Lord Jesus Christ, who with God the Father and the Holy Spirit lives and reigns for ever and ever. Amen.

Mt 2 : 1-2

A reading from a Homily of St Basil the Great.
Hom. 6 in sanctam Christi generationem: PG 31, 1471-1475.

May the joy of the Wise Men find a home in our hearts

The star came to rest over the place where the Child lay. When they saw it, the Wise Men were filled with great joy. Let us also welcome that joy of theirs into our own hearts, for it is the same as the glad tidings which the angels proclaimed to the shepherds. Let us worship the Lord with the Wise Men, glorify him with the shepherds, and join in the angels' chorus, singing: *This day is born to us a Saviour who is Christ the Lord. The Lord is our God, and he has shone upon us.* For fear of terrifying the weak he would not dazzle our eyes by appearing in the form of God, but he has come to us as a servant, in order to set free what was held in bondage. Who could be so dull of heart, so ungrateful as not to rejoice, be glad and exult with all here present? This is the festival of the whole universe, for it pours out on earth the blessings of heaven, sending the archangels to Zechariah and to Mary, and assembling the angelic choirs for their song: *Glory to God in the highest, and on earth peace, good will among men.*

The stars traverse the skies; the Wise Men journey from pagan lands, while the earth receives its Redeemer in the cave. There must be no one without some gift to offer, no one unmindful of the gratitude he owes. Let us celebrate the world's salvation, the day Christ was born in our humanity, for today Adam's sentence is reversed. No longer can it be said, *You are earth, and to the earth you shall return;* rather, 'You are now united to heaven, and to heaven you shall be admitted'. Now we no longer hear, *In sorrow you shall bring forth your children,* since happy is she who has borne Emmanuel, and happy is the breast which has nursed him. *For to us a child is born, to us a son is given, and sovereignty shall be upon his shoulder.*

Come then, and join those who gladly welcomed the Lord from heaven. Think of the shepherds now clothed with wisdom, the priests blessed with the gift of prophecy, and the women, Mary and Elizabeth, filled with happiness, the one rejoicing at Gabriel's message, the other at John's leaping in her womb. Think of Anna proclaiming the good news and Simeon holding the child in his arms. Adoring the mighty God in the tiny infant, they did not despise what they saw but praised his divine majesty. Like light shining through clear glass, the power of the Godhead shone in radiance through that human body for those whose inner gaze was pure. May the Lord grant us also to be counted among them, so that beholding his splendour with unveiled face, we may be transformed from glory to glory by the grace and loving kindness of our Lord Jesus Christ, to whom be honour and power for ever and ever.   Amen.

JANUARY 7

A reading from the sermons of St Peter Chrysologus, Bishop of Ravenna.
Sermon 160: PL 52: 620-622.

He whose will it was to be born for us
did not wish to remain unknown

Although the presence of the godhead was at all times clearly evident in the mystery of the Word made flesh, the solemnity of the Epiphany gives us many more indications that God has come in a human body. For our mortal nature is continually shrouded in darkness, and without such proofs it might in its ignorance fail to recognize what grace alone makes it capable of possessing. He whose will it was to be born for us did not wish to remain unknown. Therefore, to prevent the great mystery of his loving kindness becoming for us the occasion of grave error, he manifested his incarnation to us by the signs which we celebrate today.

The first is that after searching the stars for his appearance in glory, the Wise Men find him in a cradle: a crying baby. They marvel at the sight of this Child, shown to them in swaddling clothes, who has for so long been hidden from them amid the constellations of heaven. Lost in wonder, they ponder over what they gaze upon: heaven on earth, earth taken up to heaven; man in God, God in man; what the whole world cannot encompass, contained in a tiny body. From the moment they see him, they believe without question. The gifts they offer proclaim their faith: incense for God, gold for a king, myrrh for one who is to die.

Through their action the Gentiles have moved from the last place to the first, since today, in the Wise Men's profession of faith, pagan credulity has been consecrated to the truth.

Today we also commemorate Christ's going down into the waters of the Jordan, to wash away the sin of the world. For this is why he has come, as John himself bears witness in the words: *Behold the Lamb of God, who takes away the sins of the world.* Today a servant restrains his Lord, man touches God, John lays his hand upon Christ — not to grant forgiveness, but to receive it.

Today, as the prophet says, *The voice of the Lord is heard over the waters* — the voice that declares, *This is my beloved Son, in whom I am well pleased.* Today the Holy Spirit broods over the waters in the form of a dove. As in the time of the Deluge Noah learned from a dove that the flood had subsided upon the earth, so now, by the same sign, we know that the world has been saved from everlasting destruction. But here, unlike Noah's dove which brought him a branch of an ancient olive tree, the Holy Spirit pours out all the riches of a new anointing upon the head of the Father of the world to come. So the prophecy is fulfilled: *God, your God has anointed you with the oil of gladness, above all your companions.*

Finally we recall today that when he changed water into wine Christ worked the first of his heavenly signs. But water was destined to be changed into the sacrament of his Blood, so that from the vessel of his own body he might give pure wine to those who would drink. Thus he would fulfil the prophet's words: *My cup is overflowing; how magnificent it is!*

JANUARY 8

A reading from an Epiphany Sermon attributed to St Hippolytus. 2. 6-8. 10: PG 10, 853. 857. 860. 861.

Water and the Spirit

What an astonishing thing it was for Jesus to come and receive baptism in the Jordan at the hands of John! The endless river that gives joy to the city of God, bathed in a poor little stream! The bottomless well whose unfailing waters are the source of life for all men, immersed in a trickle of water that would one day disappear! He who fills all creation, leaving no place devoid of his presence, he who is incomprehensible to angels, invisible to men, came of his own free will to be baptized. *And behold, the heavens were opened to him, and a voice said: This is my beloved son in whom I am well pleased.*

The Beloved calls forth love, and divine Light radiates divine, unapproachable Light. He is called the son of Joseph, but in his divine nature he is my Only-begotten. *This is my beloved son.* He knew hunger, while feeding thousands; he toiled, while giving rest to the toil-worn; he had nowhere to lay his head, while his hand upheld the universe; he suffered, while healing the wounds of men; he received the blow on the cheek, while giving freedom to the whole world; He was pierced in the side, while redeeming the fault that sprang from Adam's side.

Now I beg you to give me your full attention, for I want to return to that life-giving fountain, and contemplate its healing waters at their Source. The immortal Father sent his immortal Son and Word into the world. He came to us men to baptize us with water and the Spirit; and in order to give us a new birth that would render both our souls and bodies immortal, he breathed into us the breath of life, investing us with incorruptibility. Now if we become immortal, we shall also become divine; if we become divine after baptismal regeneration through water and the Holy Spirit, we shall also be joint-heirs with Christ after the resurrection from the dead.

So my cry is this: Come peoples of the earth, and receive the immortality that flows from baptism. By this water, united to the Spirit, paradise is irrigated, earth is made fertile, plants grow, animals bring forth their young; in short, by this water regenerate man is given life, in it Christ was baptized, into it the Spirit descended in the form of a dove.

Everyone who, with faith, goes down into this bath of regeneration, renounces the devil and joins himself to Christ. He repudiates the Enemy, and confesses Christ to be God; he throws off his servitude, and is raised to filial status. He comes up from his baptism bright as the sun, radiant in his purity; much more, he comes up a son of God and co-heir with Christ. To him and to his good, holy and life-giving Spirit be glory and power now and always, throughout all ages, amen.

JANUARY 9

A reading from the Sermons of St Proclus, Patriarch of Constantinople.
On the Feast of the Holy Epiphany, Sermon 7, 1-3: PG 65, 757-760.

The Sanctification of the Waters

Christ gave joy to our world at his appearance, for he brought all its discords into harmony; he took its sin upon himself and overthrew its Enemy; he made holy its springs of water, and flooded with his light the souls of men. Wonder followed wonder, each more amazing than the last. For today land and sea share the Saviour's grace, and the whole world is filled with gladness. Today's feast, more clearly than the one we lately celebrated, demonstrates the multiplication of marvels. Then, at our Saviour's birth, earth had its joy, for it cradled in the manger the Lord of the universe. But today, on the feast of the Lord's baptism, the sea rejoices to share in the sanctification of the Jordan. On the former festival, the sight of a new-born babe reminded us of our own human imperfection: on today's feast, the contemplation of that babe now grown to full maturity, raises our minds to him who proceeds in divine perfection from the all-perfect God. Then the King was wrapped in the purple robe of flesh: now the Fountain-head is immersed in the waters of a river.

Come then, behold an undreamt-of marvel: the Sun of Righteousness bathed in the Jordan; fire submerged in water; God sanctified by man. Today the whole of creation resounds with the song of praise: *Blessed is he who comes in the name of the Lord*. Blessed is he who is always coming: not for the first time has he come among us now.

But who has come? Tell us clearly, blessed David: *The Lord is our God, and he has appeared to us*. Nor is the prophet David the only one to say so, for his statement is borne out by the Apostle Paul: *The grace of God has appeared*, he announces, *to bring salvation to all mankind, and to instruct us.* Not only to a select few, but to all: there are no bounds to the benefits of baptism. Through it, salvation is freely bestowed upon everyone, whether he be Jew or Greek.

Come and see this amazing new flood. Far wider its expanse, mightier its torrent, than the one the days of Noah saw. Then the flood waters destroyed the human race: today, through the power of him who is himself baptized, the waters of baptism have brought the dead to life. Then a dove carrying an olive branch betokened the fragrance of Christ our Lord: today the Holy Spirit, coming in the form of a dove, signifies his mercy.

JANUARY 10

A reading from the Commentary on the Gospel of St John by St Cyril of Alexandria.
Book 4, Chapter 2: PG 73. 751-754.

The Holy Spirit poured out upon all mankind

The Creator of the universe, desiring to restore the nature of man to its primeval innocence, conceived the magnificent plan of gathering up all things in Christ. Accordingly one of the promises he made to man was to restore to him the Holy Spirit, since only through the Spirit could he regain the security in which he had once enjoyed the blessings of God. The time for this descent of the Spirit upon us was, by God's decree, to concur with the coming of Christ: God gave his word that in those days — by which he meant the days of our Saviour — he would pour out his Spirit upon all mankind.

So it was that when those days of his great generosity arrived, and brought down to earth in human flesh his Only-begotten

Son, a man born of woman, as the Holy Scriptures tell us, God the Father began once again to give the Spirit. Christ received it first, because he was the First-fruits of our renewed nature, and John bore witness to this, reporting that he had seen the Spirit descend from heaven and remain on him.

Now Christ is said to have received the Spirit because he had become man, and as man it was fitting for him to receive it. For the same reason, although he was the Son of God the Father, and begotten of the Father's substance even before the Incarnation, indeed before all ages, he was in no way grieved when God the Father said to him after he had become man: *You are my Son, this day have I begotten you.*

For he who before all ages was begotten by God, and was God, was begotten today, we are told, in order to receive us into himself, and so make us adopted sons of God. This was possible because Christ's being Man made the whole of humanity one man in him. So also, although the Son was already in possession of his own Spirit, the Father is said to give it to him again in order that, in him, we might receive it. This therefore was the reason for his taking descent from Abraham, and being made in all respects like his brothers.

Not for himself then did God's Only-begotten Son receive the Holy Spirit, which was his own Spirit, and was in him, and given through him. No; it was for the whole human race which he contained in himself through his having become Man, and which he intended to refashion through the Holy Spirit, and so restore it to its original innocence. That Christ did not receive the Spirit for himself, but for us in himself, is shown by right reasoning confirmed by the words of Holy Scripture, for this and every other grace comes to us through him.

JANUARY 11

A reading from the Sermons of St Maximus, Bishop of Turin.
Sermon 100 on the Epiphany, 1, 3. CCL 23: 398-400.

The mystery of our Lord's Baptism

The gospel tells us that the Lord came to the Jordan to be
baptized, and that it was his own will that he should be consecrated in its waters by signs from heaven.

It is right that this feast should follow immediately after the
birth of our Lord, for even though there was an interval of
several years between the two events, they occurred at the same
time of year, and so I think we can still say we are celebrating
the feast of the Nativity.

For at Christmas Jesus was born among men; today in baptism
he enters upon a new stage of his life. At his Incarnation he was
brought forth by the Virgin; today he is baptized into his saving
mission. At his human birth Mary his mother held him in her
arms; today when he is initiated into his messianic task, God
the Father acknowledges him as his Son, saying : *This is my Son,
in whom I am well pleased; listen to him.* So, then, his mother
caresses her baby at her gentle breast; his Father gives a paternal
testimony to him. His mother, I say, lifts him up to receive the
worship of the Wise Men; his Father reveals him to the nations
for their adoration.

Accordingly, the Lord Jesus came to be baptized, desiring to
have his sacred body washed in the waters. It may be asked why
he who is holiness itself should wish to be baptized. My answer,
if you will listen, is that Christ was baptized not in order to be
sanctified by the waters, but rather that they should be sanctified
by him, and the river purified by his contact with it. It was the
elements that received consecration, far more than Christ. For
when our Saviour was baptized, all water was made clean for

the baptism of us men, purified at its source for the dispensing of baptismal grace to the people who would follow him. Christ therefore came to be baptized first, so that Christians might follow him without hesitation.

Here I perceive a mystery: the pillar of fire went ahead of the children of Israel across the Red Sea, so that they might tread the same path undaunted; it was the first to walk through the waters, in order to mark the route for those who followed it. This event, the apostle tells us, was a type of baptism; and it was indeed a kind of baptism for men to be protected by a cloud and borne across the sea.

But all these things have been accomplished anew by Christ our Lord, who now goes to be baptized ahead of the Christian people in the pillar of his body, just as of old he crossed the sea at the head of the children of Israel in the pillar of fire. I repeat: this same pillar, which in those days gave light to the people as they marched behind it, now gives light to the hearts of the faithful. Then it made a dry path through the waves of the sea; now, in the waters of baptism, it gives men the strength to walk by faith.

JANUARY 12

A reading from the Sermons of Faustus, Bishop of Riez.
Sermon 5, On the Epiphany 2: PLS 3, 560-562.

The wedding of Christ and the Church

On the third day there was a wedding. What does this wedding signify, and what is the mystical interpretation of the number three? Surely it is the joyful pledge of man's salvation, celebrated on the third day by his profession of faith in the Trinity and his belief in the Resurrection.

113

There is another Gospel passage which describes the songs, dances and wedding garments which greeted the younger son on his return. Here the conversion of the Gentiles is signified.

Like a bridegroom coming from his tent, therefore, the incarnate Lord comes down to earth for his wedding with the Church, gathered from among the nations. He gives her both ring and dowry: the ring when the godhead is joined to humanity, the dowry when he is offered in sacrifice for our salvation. By the first we can understand our redemption in this world, and by the second our life in the world to come.

Those who witnessed the changing of water into wine saw a miracle take place; but for those who were able to understand it assumed a sacramental significance. If we look carefully, we can see a certain likeness of baptism and regeneration in the water itself. For we see one thing becoming another; by a hidden mutation we see a lower creature being transformed into a higher. In the same way the mystery of our second birth is enacted. Water undergoes a sudden change; it will be water's destiny to change men.

By the act of Christ in Galilee water becomes wine: the Law passes away and is succeeded by grace. The shadow fades and truth appears; the flesh gives way to the Spirit; the old observance is transferred to the new covenant. In the words of the blessed Apostle: *Former things have passed away; see, all is made new.* As the water contained in the jars was not diminished in quantity but began a new mode of existence, so the coming of Christ did not destroy the Law but brought it to fulfilment.

When the wine fails, therefore, another wine is provided. The wine of the old covenant was indeed good, but the new is better. The old covenant which the Jews observed has become a dead letter; the new covenant which is given to us breathes the living fragrance of grace.

The good wine is the good commandment of the Law, which you are given when you hear it said: *You shall love your neighbour, and hate your enemy.* The better and stronger vintage is the wine of the Gospel, given you with the words: *But I say to you, love your enemies, and do good to those who hate you.*

FEAST OF THE BAPTISM OF THE LORD

Sunday occurring after January 6

A reading from the Sermons of St Gregory Nazianzen.
Oratio 39 in sancta Lumina, 14-16. 20: PG 36, 350-351, 354, 358-359.

The baptism of Christ

Today Christ experiences baptismal enlightenment; let us also experience it with him. He is baptized; let us go down with him into the waters, so that we may come up from them with him.

As John is baptizing, Jesus presents himself. He comes, perhaps, to sanctify the very man baptizing him, certainly to bury the old Adam completely in the waters. In preparation for us and for our sake he hallows the Jordan, for being himself spirit and flesh he is to baptize with the Spirit and with water.

The Baptist demurs; Jesus contends with him. *It is I who should be baptized by you,* says the lantern to the Sun, the voice to the Word, the friend to the Bridegroom, the greatest born of woman to the Firstborn of every creature, he who leaped in his mother's womb to the unborn Child who received his adoration, he who was his forerunner and shall come before him again to the one who revealed himself and shall do so again.

It is I who should be baptized by you; and for you, let us add, for he knew in advance that his own baptism would be by martyrdom, and that, like Peter, it was not only his feet that he would have washed clean.

Jesus comes up out of the water, and raises up the whole world with him. He sees the heavens rent open, which Adam had barred for himself and posterity even as paradise was barred by the flaming sword, and the Spirit coming to meet him, bearing witness to the godhead they both share. The voice comes from heaven, because it was from heaven that he came to whom the witness is borne. Taking bodily shape in honour of that body which is itself divine by reason of its union with the divine nature, the Spirit appears as a dove, even as long ago, so we have been told, a dove announced the ending of the flood.

Let us pay homage this day to the baptism of Christ; let us keep the feast with fitting celebrations. We must be wholly purified and keep ourselves pure, for God delights in nothing so much as the amendment and salvation of men, for whose benefit are his every word and all his mysteries. Then we shall be like lights in the world, having power to give life to other men. Once we have received the heavenly illumination that is given in baptism, we ourselves become shining lights in the train of the supreme Light. We have a fuller and clearer understanding of divine truths than had hitherto been granted us, and the source of this enlightenment is the Trinity, whose one light radiates from the one godhead in Christ Jesus our Lord, to whom be glory and power for ever and ever.   Amen.

YEAR I. Mt 3 : 13-17

A reading from a Homily of St Gregory the Wonderworker.
Hom IV in Sancta Theophania, PG 37, 1181B-1183A.

It is I who need to be baptized by you

*I am the voice of one crying in the wilderness, Prepare the way
of the Lord.* How then can I remain silent in your presence,
Lord? Surely *it is I who need to be baptized by you, and do you
come to me?* In childhood I received from you the gift of working miracles: my birth took away my mother's barrenness and
my infant cries healed my father's dumbness. But when you
were born, in a manner known and willed by you alone, you
did not take away the maidenhood of your virgin mother Mary.
On the contrary, you guarded it intact, adding to it the title of
motherhood. Her virginity was no more impaired by your birth
than your birth was hindered by her virginity. Rather, virginity
and childbearing, though contrary to one another, met and
formed a single bond at your nativity. Was there anything
difficult in this for the Author of nature? Mere man that I am,
I possess no more than a share in the grace of God; but you are
both God and man, the most tender lover of the human race.

*It is I who need to be baptized by you, and do you come to
me?* From the very beginning you were in existence; you were
with God and you were God, the splendour of the Father's glory,
perfect image of the all-perfect Father. You were the true light
that enlightens every man who comes into the world; and being
in the world already, you have come to that place where you
have always been. O you who in taking our flesh suffered no
change in your godhead; who dwelt among us and appeared to
your servants in the likeness of a servant; who in your divine
person became the bride which joined heaven to earth — do
you come to me? You, so great, to such as I? King to herald,
master to servant? Perhaps you were not ashamed to be born

within the lowly confines of our human nature; yet it is impossible for me to go beyond its bounds.

Between the earth and its creator, between the clay and the potter, the difference is infinite, and I know it. Sun of Justice, how your radiance outshines the glimmer of my poor candle, which owes its light to your grace alone! Though your divinity is veiled by your body as by a spotless cloud, yet I perceive and acknowledge your sovereignty. I confess my own condition as servant; I proclaim your greatness. I admit your full and perfect authority; I recognize my own unworthiness. I am not fit to stoop down and untie the thong of your sandal; how could I dare to touch your sacred head? Shall I stretch out my hand over you, when you stretch out the heavens like a tent and set the earth upon the waters? Could I lay a servant's hands upon the divine head, or wash the immaculate and sinless one? Is it for me to enlighten the light itself, pronouncing my baptismal formula over you, when you are the God who graciously receives the prayers even of those who do not know you?

YEAR I. Mt 3 : 13-17

Alternative reading

A reading from St Hilary's Commentary on Matthew.
Cap 2, 4-5: PL 9, 926-927.

Jesus has fulfilled in himself the whole mystery of our salvation

He will baptize you in the Holy Spirit and in fire. By this declaration, John the Baptist indicated the time of our salvation and judgment, for after our baptism in the Holy Spirit it still remains for us to be perfected by the fire of divine judgment.

His winnowing fork is in his hand, to clear his threshing-floor and gather the wheat into his granary. But the chaff he will burn with unquenchable fire. The winnowing fork is needed to separate good grain from worthless. In the Lord's hand it signifies his power of discernment; by its exercise he will gather into his granary those who have borne the perfect fruit of faith, and consign to the fires of judgment the worthless who are barren and bear no good fruit.

Then Jesus came from Galilee to the Jordan to be baptized by John. The whole human race was present in Christ Jesus, and consequently he fulfilled in himself, through the body which he had taken for the service of the Spirit, the whole mystery of our salvation. He came then to John, born of a woman, subject to the law, as the Word made flesh. He himself had no need of baptism, for it is written of him, *He committed no sin,* and where there is no sin there is nothing to be forgiven. But he had taken to himself a human body, and so had become a member of the human family; and thus, though he himself had no need of cleansing, it was through him that washing with water was to become the instrument of our purification. Knowing him to be God, John refused to baptize him; but he taught us that it had to be so, for only through his manhood could all righteousness be accomplished, only through him could the law be fulfilled. Although according to the prophet's testimony he did not need to be washed, he perfected the mystery of our salvation by the power of his example, sanctifying men by taking their own nature and by undergoing the baptism of water for their sake.

The heavenly mystery was revealed in due order. When Jesus was baptized the heavens were opened, the Holy Spirit was sent forth, seen in visible form as a dove, and thus Christ received the anointing of the Father's love. Then came a voice from heaven saying, *You are my Son, today I have begotten you.* By word and by vision he was revealed as the Son of God. The Lord sent to a people lacking in faith and disobedient to the prophets a testimony they could both see and hear. Therefore through what was accomplished in Christ we may realize that when we ourselves are baptized the heavens are opened, the Spirit comes down on us and we are anointed with heavenly glory as the voice of the Father makes us his adopted sons. Thus what took place in the Jordan was a true prefiguration of what the sacrament effects in us.

YEAR 2. Mk 1 : 6b-11

A reading from a homily of St Gregory of Antioch.
Hom 2 De Baptismo Christi, 5, 6, 9, 10; PG 88, 1875-1879, 1882-1883.

This is my beloved Son, in whom I am well pleased

This is my beloved Son, in whom I am well pleased. This is he who did not leave my side when he took up his dwelling in Mary's womb; he was neither separated from me, nor confined within her. Whole and undivided in heaven, he suffered no violation when he made his home in the Virgin's womb.

There are not two persons — my Son and the son of Mary : one lying in a cave and the other adored by wise men; one baptized, and the other with no need of baptism. No, this is my Son, my only Son. He who is the object of your thoughts is also the object of your bodily sight; one and the same, invisible God yet beheld by you; belonging both to eternity and to time; one with me in Godhead, and one with your human condition in all things but sin alone.

He is the mediator between me and his fellow-servants, because in his own person he restores sinners to unity with me. Son of God and Lamb of God, priest and victim, offerer and offering — he is himself the sacrifice and the one who receives it.

Such was the Father's testimony to his only-begotten Son at the time of his baptism in the Jordan. And, when Christ was transfigured on the mountain in the presence of his disciples, his face radiant with such splendour that the sunlight was dimmed, the same voice again testified: *This is my beloved Son, in whom I am well pleased: listen to him.*

If he says, *I am in the Father and the Father is in me*, listen to him. If he says, *He who has seen me has seen the Father also*, listen to him as to one who is telling the truth. If he says, *The Father who sent me is greater than I*, put this statement in the context of his divine self-abasement. If he says, *This is my Body which is broken for you for the remission of sins*, look at the body which he shows you, behold what he took from among you and made his own — now broken for you. If he says, *This is my Blood*, realize that it is the very blood of him who is speaking to you, not of some other.

We have been called by God to peace and not to conflict; let us, then, be steadfast in our calling. With the greatest reverence let us venerate the holy altar where we take part in the heavenly mysteries. Let us not be fellow-guests at this table yet at the same time stumbling-blocks to one another; sharers in the Eucharist here in church, yet, outside, inflamed with discord; otherwise the Lord may say of us, *I have begotten sons and reared them, I have fed my own kindred, but they have rejected me.*

May he who is the Saviour of all, the Author of peace, grant tranquillity to his Church and watch over this holy flock of his. May he himself protect the pastor of the flock, and bring together into his one sheepfold the sheep that stray, so that there may be but one flock, one sheepfold. To him be glory and power till time is no more. Amen.

Alternative reading

A reading from the Hymns of St Ephrem the Deacon.

Hymn 14 for the feast of the Epiphany, 6-8. 14. 32. 36-37. 47-50.

The whole world has become radiant in the light of the Lord's manifestation

Today the Source of all the graces of baptism comes himself to be baptized in the river Jordan, there to make himself known to the world. Seeing him approach, John stretches out his hand to hold him back, protesting: 'Lord, by your own baptism you sanctify all men; yours is the true baptism, the source of perfect holiness. How can you wish to submit to mine?'

But the Lord replies, 'I wish it to be so. Come and baptize me; do as I wish, for surely you cannot refuse me. Why do you hesitate, why are you so afraid? Do you not realize that the baptism I ask for is mine by every right? By my baptism the waters will be sanctified, receiving from me fire and the Holy Spirit. Unless I am immersed in them they will never be empowered to bring forth sons to eternal life. There is every reason for you to let me have my way and do what I am asking you to do. Did I not baptize you when you were in your mother's womb? Now it is your turn to baptize me in the Jordan. So come, then, carry out your appointed task.'

To this John answers, 'Your servant is utterly helpless. Saviour of all men, have mercy on me! I am not fit even to unfasten your sandal straps, let alone to lay my hand upon your venerable head. But I hear your command, Lord, and in obedience to your word I come to give you that baptism to which your own love impels you. Man of dust that I am, let deepest reverence enfold me when I behold the height to which I have been called — even to laying my hand on the head of my Maker!'

See the hosts of heaven hushed and still, as the all-holy Bridegroom goes down into the Jordan. No sooner is he baptized than he comes up from the waters, his splendour shining forth over the earth. The gates of heaven are opened, and the Father's voice is heard: *This is my beloved Son, in whom I am well pleased*. All who are present stand in awe as they watch the Spirit descend to bear witness to him. O come, all you peoples, worship him! Praise to you, Lord, for your glorious Epiphany which brings joy to us all! The whole world has become radiant with the light of your manifestation.

YEAR 3. Lk 3 : 15-16, 21-22

A reading from an Epiphany Sermon attributed to St Hippolytus. PG 10: 858-859.

Come and receive the immortality that flows from baptism

When Jesus had come up out of the water after being baptized, immediately the heavens were opened to him and the Spirit of God descended in the form of a dove and rested upon him; and a voice from heaven said : This is my beloved Son in whom I am well pleased.

Suppose, beloved, that the Lord had yielded to John's exhortation and not received baptism. Do you see how many great blessings we should have been deprived of? Until then the heavens had been closed, our homeland on high inaccessible. Once having descended into the depths of sin we could no longer raise our minds to heavenly things. Was it only the Lord who was baptized? By no means; he also renewed our fallen nature, even going so far as to restore us to our former status as sons. For *immediately the heavens were opened to him*. The world we see was reconciled with that which lies beyond our vision; the

123

angels were filled with joy; earthly disorders healed; secrets unveiled; enmity was turned into friendship. *The heavens were opened to him,* we are told. Why? For three reasons that fill us with amazement. The heavenly bridal-chamber was bound to fling wide its shining doors for Christ at his baptism, for he was the bridegroom. So also the gates of heaven had to be lifted up for the Holy Spirit to descend in the form of a dove, and for the voice of the Father to resound near and far. *The heavens were opened to him, and a voice said : This is my beloved Son, in whom I am well pleased.*

The Beloved calls forth Love, and divine Light radiates divine, unapproachable Light. *This is my beloved Son* who, without leaving his Father, appeared on earth in visible form. But that outward appearance did not reveal his inner being; in fact it was misleading, for it made him seem, as the one baptized, inferior to John who baptized him. This is why the Father sent the Holy Spirit down on him from heaven. In Noah's ark God's love for man was revealed by the dove; so also now the Spirit descended in the form of a dove as though bearing an olive branch, and rested on him to whom witness was borne. Why? So that the Father's voice should be recognized, and the ancient prophecy believed. What prophecy? *The voice of the Lord sounded upon the waters, the God of glory thundered, the Lord thundered upon many waters.* And his message? *This is my beloved Son, in whom I am well pleased.* You call him the son of Joseph, but in his divine nature he is my Only-begotten. *This is my beloved Son.* He knew hunger, while feeding millions; he toiled, while giving rest to the toil-worn; he had nowhere to lay his head, while his hand upheld the universe; he suffered, while healing the wounds of men; he received the blow on the cheek, while giving freedom to the whole world; he was pierced in the side, while redeeming the fault that sprang from Adam's side.

Now I beg you to give me your full attention, for I want to

return to that life-giving fountain, and contemplate its healing waters at their Source. The immortal Father sent his immortal Son and Word into the world. He came to us men to baptize us with water and the Spirit; and in order to give us a new birth that would render both our souls and bodies immortal, he breathed into us the breath of life, investing us with incorruptibility. Now if we become immortal, we shall also become divine; if we become divine after baptismal regeneration through water and the Holy Spirit, we shall also be joint-heirs with Christ after the resurrection from the dead.

So my cry is this: Come, peoples of the earth, and receive the immortality that flows from baptism. I bring the good news of life to you, who, up to now, have wandered aimlessly in the darkness of ignorance. Come from servitude to freedom, from the tyrant's yoke to kingly glory, from corruptibility to immortality. 'How shall we come', you ask? How? By water and the Holy Spirit. By this water, united to the Spirit, paradise is irrigated, earth is made fertile, plants grow, animals bring forth their young; in short, by this water regenerate man is given life, in it Christ was baptized, into it the Spirit descended in the form of a dove.

Lk 3: 15-16, 21-22

Alternative reading

A reading from Tertullian's Treatise on Baptism.
8, 3-9, 2: Edit. CCL 1, 283-284.

Never does Christ appear without water

Once our bodies have been cleansed and blessed, the Holy Spirit gladly comes down upon them from the Father, and hovers over the waters of baptism as though recognizing his primeval place. It was he who came down upon the Lord in the form of a dove, in order that his own nature might be mirrored in the simplicity and innocence of a creature that has no gall. Hence the Lord tells us to be simple as doves, words that contain an allusion to an Old Testament figure. For after the waters of the flood had washed away the world's ancient sin — one might call this its baptism — the dove which was released from the ark returned with an olive branch, to show that the anger of heaven was appeased. This token is held out as a sign of peace even to the pagans. In a similar but spiritual manner, the dove representing the Holy Spirit is sent from heaven where the Church is — the Church of which the ark was the type — and flies down to earth bearing God's peace. In other words, the Holy Spirit rests upon our bodies as they emerge from the font in which our former sins have been washed away.

How many are the endowments of nature, prerogatives of grace, solemn rites, types, preparations, prophecies, which have determined the sacred use of water! In the first place, when the Israelites escaped from Pharoah's violence by passing through water, those same waters destroyed him together with his entire army. What could be a clearer figure of the sacrament of baptism? The nations are set free from slavery to this world by means of the water in which they leave their old tyrant, the devil, to drown. Again, bitter waters were restored to sweetness by the wood which Moses threw into them. That wood was Christ, who himself changes the bitter springs of our poisoned nature into the all-healing waters of baptism. This was the stream which gave drink to the people from the rock accompanying them; for if the rock is Christ, we can see that baptism undoubtedly derives its consecration from the water whose source is in him. What immense grace water must possess with God and his Christ to corroborate the baptismal rite!

Never does Christ appear without water. He was himself baptized in it. It was through water that he showed the first sign of his divine power at the marriage feast. In his preaching he called all who thirst to the water of eternal life. When he spoke of love, he numbered among the works of charity the giving of a cup of cold water to one's neighbour. He recruited his strength by resting beside a well. He walked on water, freely crossed the sea, washed the feet of his disciples with water. And water continued to bear its witness even in his Passion. When he was condemned to the cross, water played its part, as Pilate's hands can testify; and when he was pierced by the soldier's lance, water gushed forth from his side.

YEAR 3. Lk 3 : 15-16, 21-22

Alternative reading

A reading from a Homily of St Gregory Palamas.
Hom 16: PG 151, 198-199.

> *When Jesus was baptized and was praying,*
> *the heavens were opened*

When the time had come for the revelation and open presentation of that plan of salvation which surpasses all human expression, God sent forth John, surnamed the Precursor, from the desert. He baptized those who came to him, exhorting them to be ready to believe in the One who was to come, who would baptize them in the Holy Spirit and in fire, and teaching them that as the Holy Spirit is greater than water, so the One who was to come would rank higher than himself. He bore witness that the expected Messiah was the Lord and Creator of all things, master of both men and angels. All mankind would be his spiritual harvest-field, and for its winnowing his hand would control the powers of public authority. Not by his own testimony alone did John declare the greatness of the one to come, but he pointed to Isaiah also as a herald of the Lord. By contrast, he described himself as a servant sent to announce his master's coming, and to urge the faithful to prepare their hearts to receive him. *I*, he declared, *am the voice of one crying in the wilderness, Prepare the way of the Lord.*

So Christ himself, in obedience to him who had sent John, came to be baptized. *It is fitting*, he said, *for us to conform to custom in this way.* His baptism was to be his manifestation to Israel. Since he came to open the way of salvation and make it secure for all the baptized who would follow him, he himself had to be the first in whom the gift of the Spirit should be revealed. He instituted the sacrament of baptism for the cleansing of that deep-rooted defilement within us which stems from our earthly, fallen birth and sinful manner of life. Christ himself, as man, had no need to be cleansed, for he had been born of the Immaculate Virgin and was free from sin throughout his life; yet, having become man for us, for our sake he was also purified. He was baptized, therefore, by John. As he came up from the water the heavens opened above him and the Father's voice was heard, *This is my beloved Son, in whom I am well pleased*, while the Spirit of God descended upon him like a dove. Thus was revealed to the bystanders the significance of the man to whom heaven had testified.

A reading from the Sermons of St Anselm.
Oratio 52: PL 158, 955-956.

Virgin, in whose blessing every nature is blessed

The sky and the stars rejoice; the earth and the waters rejoice; day and night rejoice; all things subject to man, all things appointed for his service rejoice, O Mary, that you have been the means of restoring their lost beauty and filling them with new and ineffable grace.

It is as if they had all suffered a kind of death, losing the dignity of their true nature, which is to be of service to those who praise God, the purpose of their creation. For they were violated and defaced, in being used by those who bow down to idols, since for this they were not created. They seem, however, to rejoice in a new-found life, now that they are ruled over by those who acknowledge God, and receive beauty from being used by them. But it was as if they exulted with a new and inestimable grace when, not only did they experience the invisible rule of God the Creator himself, but they even saw him present among them in visible form, making them holy by his use of them.

These mighty things came to pass for our world through the blessed fruit of the womb of Mary, the blessed one.

Through the fullness of your grace, O Lady, things of the underworld rejoiced at their liberation, and those on earth and above it, found bliss in their restoration. Indeed, through that same glorious Son of your resplendent virginity, all the just who died before his life-giving death exult at their release from captivity, while there is joy among the angels, because the walls of the heavenly Jerusalem, so near to ruin, are seen to rise again.

O Lady, full and more than full of grace, to you I cry praise, since that superabundance rains down to revive all creation. To you I sing hail, Virgin favoured of God and more than favoured, you in whose blessing every nature is blessed, not only creatures by their Creator, but the Creator by his own creatures!

God gave to Mary that very Son who alone is begotten in God's inner life, equal to him, and whom he loves as he loves himself. From Mary God made himself a Son, not another Son, but the very same. Thus was his purpose achieved, that, in the working of nature, one and the same should become the Son both of God and of Mary. All nature is created by God, yet God was born of Mary. God created all things, yet Mary brought forth God. Our God, who made all, made himself from Mary, and thus re-made all that he had made. He who was able to make all things out of nothing did not wish to re-make them, when they were disfigured, without Mary's co-operation.

God is therefore the Father of all created things, and Mary the mother of re-created things. God is the Father who has given universal order, Mary the Mother through whom all was restored to order. For God begot him through whom all things were made, and Mary gave birth to him through whom all things were saved. God begot him without whom nothing has being, and Mary bore him without whom nothing has well-being. *The Lord is with you* indeed, since he has ordained that Nature should owe to you the abundance of her own restored existence.

A reading from the works of St. Augustine.
De natura et gratia, cap 36, 42: PL 44, 267.

Where Mary is concerned, there can be no question of sin

When sin is in question, I will have no mention whatever of the Blessed Virgin Mary, out of reverence for the Lord. For how can we know by what extraordinary grace she was enabled utterly to vanquish sin — she who was worthy to conceive and bear him whom all agree to have been sinless?

The Virgin, then, is an exception. But if all other saints, both men and women, could have been brought together in their lifetime and asked whether they were without sin, what do you think their reply would have been? Would it have agreed with the teaching of Pelagius, or of the Apostle John? I ask you: however great their sanctity when they were in this world, if we were able to question them would they not cry out with one voice, *If we said we had no sin we should be deceiving ourselves, and denying the truth?* Is this, perhaps, the response of humility rather than truth? Not at all; by God's just decree, the merit of humility cannot be won by a lie. If their words are true, then they are sinners, and honest because they humbly admit it; if untrue, they are sinners none the less because of their untruthfulness.

DECEMBER 26
SAINT STEPHEN, THE FIRST MARTYR

A reading from the Sermons of St Fulgentius, Bishop of Ruspe.
Sermon 3, 1-3, 5-6: CCL 91A, 905-909.

The weapons of love

Yesterday we celebrated the birth in time of our eternal king; today we celebrate the triumphant suffering of a soldier. For yesterday our king, nobly arrayed in flesh, proceeding from the chaste womb of the Virgin Mary, deigned to visit the world; today a soldier, leaving the confines of the body, made his way in triumph to heaven.

Our king, though he is the Most High, for our sake came in humility; yet he could not come empty-handed. It was indeed a generous gift that he brought for his warriors, one by which he not only abundantly enriched them but gave them strength to do battle and never be vanquished. What he brought was the gift of love, which was to lead men to become sharers in the godhead. He brought it only to expend it, without in any way diminishing his own store; while turning the poverty of his liegemen into riches he remained himself, as by a miracle, fully possessed of his own inexhaustible treasury.

Love then, the same love that brought Christ down from heaven to earth, raised Stephen from earth to heaven; the same love shown first in the king was reproduced in its splendour in the warrior.

And so Stephen, in order to earn his right to the crown his name signifies, armed himself with love, and by that same love won every battle. It was love of God that made him yield not an inch to the persecuting Jews, love of his neighbour that led him to intercede for the men who stoned him. It was through love that he was able to expose those in error so that they might change their ways; through love that he prayed for those who stoned him so that they should not be punished. Trusting only in love, he overcame Saul's cruel rage, and the very man who had been his persecutor on earth he won as his companion in heaven. That same holy and untiring love longed to win over by prayer those whom it could not convert by persuasion.

See how Paul rejoices with Stephen, see how with Stephen he delights in the radiant vision of Christ; see how he exults with Stephen and reigns with him. Where Stephen went before, crushed to death by Paul's stoning, there Paul followed, aided by Stephen's prayers.

Here, surely, is the true life, my brethren, where it is not Paul who is dismayed by the killing of Stephen but Stephen who welcomes the companionship of Paul, since love rejoices in each of them. Love in Stephen prevailed over the anger of the Jews; love in Paul covered a multitude of sins; love in each alike merited possession of the kingdom of heaven. Love is therefore the source and origin of every good, an unrivalled protection, the road that leads to heaven. He who walks in love can be neither lost nor afraid; love guides him, protects him, and brings him to the end of his journey. For this reason, brethren, since Christ has set up a stairway of love by which every Christian can mount to heaven, keep a firm hold on love alone; love one another, and by growing in love climb together up to heaven.

Mt 10 : 17-22

A reading from the Sermon on the Beatitudes by St Gregory of Nyssa.
Oratio 8, PG 44: 1292-1296, 1300-1301.

Blessed are those who suffer persecution for my sake

Blessed are those who suffer persecution for my sake, for theirs is the Kingdom of Heaven. To be counted fit for the kingdom of heaven — this is the objective of all our struggles for God's sake, the reward of all our toil, the recompense for all our striving.

The Lord sees the frailty of men and tells them what the outcome of their trials will be, so that in their expectation of the kingdom the weak may easily overcome the passing experience of pain. Such was the hope which caused the great saint Stephen to rejoice at the stones which assailed him from every side. Thick and fast as hailstones they fell, but to him they were like a gentle dew to which he gladly exposed his body. Praying that the sin of his murderers might not be held against them, he answered them with blessings, because of the promise he had heard and the hope he now saw being realized. He had been assured that those who suffered persecution for the Lord's sake would enter the kingdom of heaven; when the time of his own torments came, he saw the fulfilment of his hopes. He had run the race, he had made his profession of faith, and now he was shown what he had looked forward to: heaven lying open, the Divine Majesty bending down from on high to watch his course, and the greatest of all Champions vouching for him as he ran.

There is a mysterious significance for us in this presiding Presence, for it teaches us that the Organizer of the contest is none other than the one who sides with his own men against their opponents. Could a man suffering persecution for the Lord's sake have any greater blessing than to know that he had the President of the contest as his helper?

Blessed, therefore, *are those who suffer persecution for my sake.*

Now life must be lived in a definite place. Unless we are cast out from the earth, earth remains our abode; but on our departure hence we change our dwelling place for heaven. It follows that what now seems harsh and grievous to you will become the occasion of the greatest happiness. The Apostle makes this point when he says: *Discipline is never pleasant; at the time it seems painful, but in the end it bears fruit in peace and goodness in the lives of those who have been trained by it.*

Affliction, therefore, is the blossom that comes before the longed-for fruit. We must pluck the flower for the sake of the fruit; welcome persecution, and so run our race. Let us make sure, however, that our running is not in vain. Our course must be set for the prize of our heavenly calling, and our manner of running such that we attain it. Let us not grieve, then, when we are attacked and persecuted; it is a matter rather for rejoicing, since through the assaults of those who enjoy worldly honour we are propelled towards heavenly bliss. This is the assurance of him who promised beatitude to all who suffer persecution for his sake; theirs is the kingdom of heaven, by the grace of our Lord Jesus Christ, to whom belong glory and power for ever and ever.   Amen.

Alternative reading

A reading from the Homilies of St Gregory of Nyssa.
PG 46: 721-724.

Stephen, full of grace and power

Christ came into the world to save it, and immediately afterwards the Church began to bear fruit. He shone out as witness to the truth; in his company shone those who witnessed to his great plan of salvation. His disciples followed their Master, walking in the footsteps of their Lord. After Christ came Christ-bearers; after the Sun of Justice, earth's luminaries. The first to come to full flowering was Stephen, whose name means 'garland' or 'crown'. He was a crown woven, not from the thorns of Jewry, but from the firstfruits offered by the Church to the Lord of the harvest.

As their inaugural votive offering and first produce of their husbandry, the labourers in the field of gospel truth brought to their Master the holy man Stephen, as though he were a genuine garland of many different virtues intertwined. This exemplary man was entrusted with the care of the widows, for he was attested as *a man full of faith and the Holy Spirit* both by the approval and choice of the apostles and by the power of spiritual wisdom he displayed.

His inspired words used to bear such vivid testimony to his message that his preaching was accompanied by great signs of divine power. Stephen, it is written, *full of grace and power, did great wonders and signs.* He did not regard the care of the widows as a hindrance; it was a charge he readily undertook, without ever abandoning the ministry of the word. What admiration he aroused! What a labour-loving spirit he mani-fested! The care of widows and the cure of souls — both were his concern. He provided bread for the former and instruction for the latter, material food for the one and spiritual fare for the other. A good man indeed, full of the Holy Spirit, he not only fulfilled with integrity his task of serving the poor, but by the freedom of his speech and the power of the Holy Spirit reduced the enemies of the truth to silence.

DECEMBER 27
SAINT JOHN, APOSTLE AND EVANGELIST

A reading from St Augustine's Commentary on the Letter of St. John.
Tract. 1, 1, 3: PL 35, 1978, 1980.

Life itself is revealed in the flesh

What has existed from the beginning, what we have heard, and have seen with our own eyes; what we have watched and touched with our hands : the Word, who is life — this is our subject. How could one actually touch the Word, were it not that *the Word was made flesh and dwelt among us?* Now this Word, which was made flesh and so could be handled, began to be flesh out of the flesh of the Virgin Mary; yet that was not the beginning of the Word, which he calls *something which has existed since the beginning.* Notice how what he says in his Epistle is borne out by his Gospel, which you have just heard : *In the beginning was the Word, and the Word was with God.* Everyone, perhaps, gains some knowledge of Christ by hearing in this way what amounts to a verbal expression : 'the Word of life'; but they do not receive that same body of Christ which we touch with our hands. Notice what follows : *That life was made visible.* Christ, therefore, is the Word of life. How was it made visible? True, it had *existed since the beginning,* but it was not made visible to men. It was made visible to the angels, who saw it and fed upon it as if it were their bread. But what does Scripture say? *Men ate the bread of angels.* The same Life, therefore, was made visible in the flesh, because by being made visible that Life, which can only be perceived by the heart, is presented as a reality, visible also to human eyes for the healing of hearts. For the Word is perceived only in the heart, but the flesh is also perceived by bodily vision. We were able to see the

Word, since the Word itself became flesh — which is something visible to our mortal eyes; and this was so that the heart — by which we perceived the Word — might be healed by what we saw with our eyes.

We saw it, he says, *and we are giving our testimony, telling you of the eternal life which was with the Father and has been made manifest in us,* that is: which has been made visible in us, or, to put it more clearly, visible to us.

What we have seen and heard we are telling you. Mark these words, my dear friends: what we have seen and heard we are telling you. Those disciples saw the Lord himself present in the flesh; they heard the words that came from the Lord's lips and they proclaimed them to us. We too have heard, though we have not seen. Are we for that reason less favoured than those who have both seen and heard? And why should he add: *that you too may be in union with us?* They saw him but we did not, yet we are in union with them because we share the same faith. And may our fellowship be *in union with the Father and with his Son Jesus Christ. We are writing this to you so that your joy may be complete.* He means here the fullness of joy, in that same fellowship, that same love, that same unity.

A reading from a Sermon by St Chromatius, Bishop of Aquileia.
Sermon 22, 1-3, 5: SC 164, 53-56.

The beloved disciple

The gospel tells us many great and admirable things about Saint John, whose feast we are celebrating today; but as it is impossible for us to expound them all in full, we must be content to say a little of all that could be said.

Saint John was the youngest of all the disciples; youngest, that is, in years, but he was their senior in the faith, for the gospel reckons him among the first. Whenever, in fact, the

Lord wished to select a group from among the apostles, he always included John among them. When he desired to reveal his glory to his disciples on the mountain, it was John he took together with Peter and James. These three disciples he led up the mountain by themselves, and was transfigured before them.

At the time of his Passion, when for the world's salvation the Son of God hung upon the cross, it was to none but John that he entrusted Mary his mother, saying to him: *Behold your mother*, and to her: *Behold your son.* In thus leaving his holy mother to John, he did not abandon her, for he keeps all men in his divine care; rather he showed towards her the affection of his filial love. The Lord is indeed the source of all love, and so it was right that he should show this loving affection towards Mary. In this instance again John was chosen from among all the holy apostles, because on account of the grace that was given him he was loved by Christ with a special affection.

The same saint John also wrote a gospel, the excellence and fame of which are well known to everyone. The Gospel according to John is a most necessary weapon in the refutation of all heresies, for in it Christ's divinity is plainly stated and it is shown that he is truly God. Since, then, today is the birthday of so great and distinguished an apostle, let us celebrate his feast with fitting honour, so that with the help of his prayers we may reach that eternal glory which God has prepared for his saints.

A reading from the Sermons on the Gospel of St John by St Augustine.
Sermon 36. 1, 2: PL 35. 1662, 1663.

In the beginning was the Word

St John is the Apostle whose symbol is the eagle, an appropriate symbol for one with such a piercing insight into the things of the spirit. In the four Gospels, or rather in the four books that make up the one Gospel, it was St John who, in his teaching, soared to heights far loftier than those attained by the other three Evangelists, and it was his wish to carry our hearts with him on his flight. The other three walked with the Lord as with a man upon the earth, and said little concerning his divinity. But John, as though scorning to tread upon earth, rose, by his very first words, not only above the earth, above the atmosphere, above the heavens, but even above the whole army of angels and all the array of invisible Powers. Then, reaching him through whom all things were made, he thundered out : *In the beginning was the Word, and the Word was with God, and the Word was God; he was in the beginning with God. All things were made through him, and without him nothing was made.*

The sublimity of this beginning was well matched by all that followed, for John spoke of the divinity of our Lord as no other has ever spoken. He himself drank in our Lord's teaching and then passed it on to us, for not without reason does this same Gospel tell how, when they were at supper, he reclined upon the Lord's breast. Secretly from that source he drank, and what he secretly drank in he openly proclaimed, for he wished to bring to all nations the news not only of the Incarnation of the Son of God, and of his Passion and Resurrection, but also of what he was before the Incarnation : the only Son of the Father, the Father's co-eternal Word, the equal of him by whom he was sent, even though his being sent made him less, so that the Father should have precedence.

Therefore, whenever you hear some statement concerning the Lord Jesus Christ as he was in his condition of lowliness, think of the divine dispensation that led him to take upon himself our human nature; think of what he became to save us, not of what he was when he made us. But when you hear or read in the Gospel sublime descriptions of him that show his exaltation above all creatures, his divinity, his equality and co-eternity with the Father, know then that what you are reading pertains, not to his condition as a servant, but to his Godhead.

If you never depart from this rule, those of you who can understand it — those who cannot will have to take it on faith — if you never depart from this rule, I say, then you will have nothing to fear in your struggle against the calumnies of heretics who walk in darkness, for you will be walking in the light.

DECEMBER 28
THE HOLY INNOCENTS

A reading from the Sermons of St Quodvultdeus.
Sermon 2 on the Creed: PL 40, 655.

Even before they speak they are confessors of Christ

A great king is born as a little child. The wise men are drawn to him from afar; they come to worship him who even as he lies here in the manger reigns over heaven and earth. When the wise men announce the birth of a King, Herod is troubled, and for fear of losing his kingdom seeks to kill the child; whereas if he would only believe in him he would reign in safety here and in the life to come for ever.

What have you to fear, Herod, when you hear that a King is born? He has not come to destroy you but to conquer the devil. But not understanding this you are in a turmoil and give vent to your rage; and in order to destroy the one child you seek, you make yourself a monster of cruelty by killing all those others. You are swayed by no compassion for the mothers' tears and the fathers' grief at their children's fate, nor by the crying and wailing of the little ones themselves. You make victims of those little bodies because your own heart is the victim of fear, and you imagine that if you can accomplish your object you can live to a great age, though Life itself is what you seek to kill.

But he, who is the source of grace, little yet mighty, shakes your throne even as he lies in the manger; without your knowing it he works out his purposes through you and frees souls from slavery to the devil. He has taken his enemy's children and made them his own by adoption.

Without realizing it, these little ones die for Christ. Their parents lament the death of martyrs. He makes them his true witnesses even before they are able to speak. See how he reigns, he who came in such a manner to his kingdom! See how the Deliverer has begun his deliverance, and the Saviour his work of salvation! But you, Herod, ignorant of this, are in a turmoil and give vent to your rage, and even while you rage against the child you are already doing him homage without knowing it.

How great is the gift of grace! To what merits of theirs was it due that these infants should be victorious? As yet they cannot speak, and they are already confessors of Christ; as yet their limbs have not the agility to engage in battle, but already they carry off the palm of victory.

A reading from the Letters of St Cyprian.
Epist. 58, 6-7: CSEL t. 3, pp. 661-662.

Too young to fight, they were yet able to win a martyr's crown

The martyrdom of children marked the very beginning of Christ's life: for his name's sake, all those of two years old and under were put to death. Too young to fight, they were yet able to win a martyr's crown, and by their innocence bear witness to the innocence of all who shed their blood for Christ. When even such as these make martyrs, clearly no one is immune from the peril of persecution.

What a shameful thing it would be for Christ's servant to recoil from suffering when his Master suffered first; for us to be unwilling to endure something for our sins, when he, though sinless, endured so much for us! The Son of God suffered in order to make us sons of God; will the sons of men refuse to persevere in that sonship through suffering? If we have to bear with the world's hatred, we must remember that Christ bore it before we did. We may have to endure insults, exile, torture in this world, but the Creator and Lord of the world knew them first in harsher form, and warned us of them, saying, *If the world hates you, remember that it hated me before you. If you belonged to the world, the world would love its own. But you are not of the world; I chose you out of it, and therefore it hates you. Remember the saying I gave you, 'The servant is not greater than his master.' If they persecute me, they will persecute you also.* Our Lord and God practised all he taught, so there can be no excuse for a disciple who hears his teaching but does not act on it.

Beloved brethren, let none of you be so intimidated by the fear of future persecution or the imminent coming of Antichrist as not to be armed against all contingencies with the exhortations and precepts of the gospel and the warnings you have received from heaven. Antichrist may come, but Christ will come in his wake. The enemy may rage and storm, but our Lord will follow hard upon him to avenge our wounds and sufferings. The adversary may rage and threaten, but there is one who can deliver us from his hands. He it is whom we must fear, for none can escape his anger, as he himself has warned us in the words: *Do not fear those who kill the body, but cannot kill the soul.*

DECEMBER 29
SAINT THOMAS OF CANTERBURY

A reading from the Letters of St Thomas Becket, Archbishop of Canterbury.
Letter 74: PL 190: 533-536.

No man is crowned who has not genuinely done battle

If we are solicitous to be bishops and high priests in reality and not merely in name, and to understand the meaning of our calling, we must take care to keep our eyes on the man who was appointed by God to be High Priest for ever, and follow in his footsteps. On the altar of the cross he offered himself to the Father for our sake, and now from heaven he looks down upon our every action and intention, so that on the last day he may repay each one of us as our deeds deserve.

Having undertaken to act as his vicars on earth, we bishops have acquired the prestige and honour belonging to that title and dignity. We enjoy the temporal fruits of our spiritual labours. As successors of the Apostles and of apostolic men, we hold the highest rank in our churches. The purpose of all this is that through our ministry the supremacy of sin and death may be destroyed and the walls of Christ's Church built up through faith and increasing virtue into a holy temple in the Lord.

There are indeed many of us. At our ordination we promised to teach and feed the flock of Christ with earnest and persevering care, and in our public statements this is what we daily profess to do. If only our deeds confirmed our fidelity to our promise! Truly the harvest is great; a single labourer or even a small number would not be enough to gather it into the granary of the Lord.

Nevertheless, who would doubt that the Roman Church is

the head of all the churches and the source of Catholic doctrine? Who does not know that the keys of the kingdom of heaven were given to Peter? Is not the whole fabric of the Church being raised up on the foundation of Peter's faith and teaching authority, so that we may all reach mature manhood in the unity of faith and knowledge of the Son of God?

Many, certainly, are needed to plant and many to water, now that the Word has spread far and wide and the population vastly increased. Even in ancient times when there was only one altar, numerous teachers were required. How much more is this true of a concourse of nations for which Lebanon could not provide enough fuel, and neither Lebanon nor the whole of Judea provide enough beasts for burnt offerings! But no matter who plants or who waters, God gives the harvest only to the man who has planted in the Petrine faith and accepts the apostolic teaching. It is evident that every important question arising among the people is referred to the examination of Peter in the person of the Roman Pontiff. Under his primacy the hierarchy of Mother Church exercises the powers entrusted to it, in the sphere of responsibility to which each bishop has been called.

Finally, let us remember how our fathers worked out their salvation; how and through what trials the Church has grown and expanded; what storms have been weathered by the bark of Peter with Christ aboard her; and how the victor's crown has been won by those whose faith shone all the more brightly for their sufferings. So does the pageant of all the saints proclaim the endless truth, that no man is crowned who has not genuinely done battle.

ADVENT

—

CHRISTMASTIDE

ADVENT

A. UNTIL DECEMBER 16

YEAR 1   YEAR 2

WEEK 1

	YEAR 1	YEAR 2
Sunday	Is. 6: 1-13	Is. 1: 1-18
Monday	Is. 7: 1-17	Is. 1: 21-27; 2: 1-5
Tuesday	Is. 8: 1-18	Is. 2: 6-22; 4: 2-6
Wednesday	Is. 9: 1-7. (Heb. 8: 23b-9: 6)	Is. 5: 1-7
Thursday	Is. 10: 5-21	Is. 16: 1-5; 17: 4-8
Friday	Is. 11: 10-16	Is. 19: 16-25
Saturday	Is. 13: 1-22 (Heb. 13: 1-22a)	Is. 21: 6-12

WEEK 2

	YEAR 1	YEAR 2
Sunday	Is. 14: 1-21	Is. 22: 8-23
Monday	Is. 34: 1-17	Is. 24: 1-18
Tuesday	Is. 35: 1-10	Is. 24: 18-25: 5
Wednesday	Ruth 1: 1-22	Is. 25: 6-26: 6
Thursday	Ruth 2: 1-13	Is. 26: 7-21
Friday	Ruth 2: 14-23	Is. 27: 1-13
Saturday	Ruth 3: 1-18	Is. 29: 1-8

WEEK 3

	YEAR 1	YEAR 2
Sunday	Ruth 4: 1-22	Is. 29: 13-24
Monday	1 Chron. 17: 1-15	Is. 30: 18-26
Tuesday	Mich. 4: 1-7	Is. 30: 27-33; 31: 4-9
Wednesday	Mich. 5: 1-8. (Heb. 4: 14-5: 7)	Is. 31: 1-3; 32: 1, 8
Thursday	Mich. 7: 7-13	Is. 32: 15-33: 6
Friday	Mich. 7: 14-20	Is. 33: 7-24

148

B. FROM DECEMBER 17 UNTIL DECEMBER 24

	YEAR 1	YEAR 2
Dec. 17	Is. 40: 1-11	Is. 45: 1-13
Dec. 18	Is. 40: 12-18. 21-31	Is. 46: 1-13
Dec. 19	Is. 41: 8-20	Is. 47: 1-15
Dec. 20	Is. 41: 21-29	Is. 48: 1-11
Dec. 21	Is. 42: 10-25	Is. 48: 12-21; 49: 9b-13
Dec. 22	Is. 43: 1-13	Is. 49: 14-50: 1
Dec. 23	Is. 43: 18-28	Is. 51: 1-11
Dec. 24	Is. 44: 1-8. 21-23	Is. 51: 17-52: 2. 7-10

CHRISTMASTIDE

DECEMBER 25
THE BIRTH OF OUR LORD

Is. 11: 1-10.

SUNDAY WITHIN THE OCTAVE OF CHRISTMAS
THE HOLY FAMILY

Eph. 5: 21-6: 4.

	YEAR 1	YEAR 2
Dec. 29	Col. 1: 1-14	Cant. 1: 1-8
Dec. 30	Col. 1: 15-2: 3	Cant. 1: 9-2: 7
Dec. 31	Col. 2: 4-15	Cant. 2: 8-3: 5

JANUARY 1 : OCTAVE DAY OF CHRISTMAS :
THE SOLEMNITY OF THE VIRGIN MOTHER OF GOD

Heb. 2: 9-17.

Jan. 2	Col. 2: 16-3: 4	Cant. 4: 1-5: 1
Jan. 3	Col. 3: 5-16	Cant. 5: 2-6: 1 (Heb. 5: 2-6: 2)
Jan. 4	Col. 3: 17-4: 1	Cant. 6: 2-7: 10 (Heb. 6: 3-7: 10)
Jan. 5	Col. 4: 2-18	Cant. 7: 11-8: 7
Jan. 6	The Epiphany: Is. 60: 1-22	

JANUARY 6
THE EPIPHANY OF THE LORD

Is. 60: 1-22.

When EPIPHANY *is celebrated on Sunday, January 7 or 8*

	YEAR 1	YEAR 2
Jan. 6	Is. 42: 1-8	Is. 49: 1-9
Jan. 7	Is. 61: 1-11	Is. 54: 1-17
Jan. 7	or Monday after Epiphany. Is. 61: 1-11	Is. 54: 1-17
Jan. 8	or Tuesday after Epiphany. Is. 62: 1-12	Is. 55: 1-13
Jan. 9	or Wed. after Epiphany. Is. 63: 7-64: 1 (Heb. 63: 7-19)	Is. 56: 1-8
Jan. 10	or Thursday after Epiphany. Is. 64: 1-12 (Heb 63: 19b-64: 11)	Is. 59: 15-21
Jan. 11	or Friday after Epiphany. Is. 65: 13-25	Bar. 4: 5-29
Jan. 12	or Saturday after Epiphany. Is. 66: 5-14a, 18-23	Bar. 4: 30-5: 9

THE SUNDAY OCCURRING AFTER JANUARY 6
THE FEAST OF THE BAPTISM OF OUR LORD JESUS CHRIST

Is. 42: 1-8; 49: 1-9.

151